꧁

WRITING
THROUGH
REVELATIONS
VISIONS
AND
DREAMS

The memoir of a writer's soul

꧁

Other books by Stella Pope Duarte

Fragile Night

Let Their Spirits Dance

If I Die in Juárez

Women Who Live in Coffee Shops and Other Stories

Essays, articles, and anthology collections are accessible
on-line, or at www.stellapopeduarte.com

Author may be reached at:
spopeduarte@yahoo.com

WRITING

through

REVELATIONS,
VISIONS
and
DREAMS

The memoir of a writer's soul

STELLA POPE DUARTE

First Edition | 2012
Published by Pope Communications
Phoenix, Arizona

FIRST EDITION

Published by Pope Communications
www.stellapopeduarte.com
spopeduarte@yahoo.com

Book cover and interior designed by Yolie Hernandez | yolie@hisi.org

Duarte, Stella Pope

Writing through Revelations, Visions and Dreams: The memoir of a writer's
soul / Stella Pope Duarte —1st ed.
pp. 162

ISBN 13: 978-1479221202

1. Autobiography 2. Writing memoir 3. Creative writing process 4. Use of
dreams and imagery 5. Writing techniques 6. Phoenix, Arizona 7. Arizona-
United States

Printed in the United States of America.

Dedicated to the memory of my father,
Francisco Moreno Duarte
and my mother,
Rosanna Pope Duarte.
The dream, the vision—
it all came true.
Thank you, Mom and Dad.

Contents

Then the Lord answered me and said:
Write down the vision
clearly upon the tablets
so that one can read it readily.
For the vision still has its time,
presses on to fulfillment, and will not
disappoint;
If it delays, wait for it,
it will surely come, it will not be late.

Habakkuk 2:2-3

We are such stuff as dreams are made on; and our
little life is rounded with a sleep.

Shakespeare "The Tempest"

1

LEARNING THE LANGUAGE OF YOUR OWN SOUL

It doesn't matter what other languages you speak, as long as you understand the language of your own soul.

D ARKNESS. Eyes close, the mind drifts off to sleep, easily, at times desperately. Then light appears—nebulous, and eyes begin to "see" and ears begin to "hear" as the physical, emotional and spiritual worlds work together to create a video from within. Images appear as real as if projected on a screen, as the dreamer begins to capture internal photos of emotions, longings, secrets often not known to the conscious mind, hopes, joys, pain, turmoil, and inclinations of things to come. As images appear instantaneously, they disappear just as quickly with lightening speed that cannot be accurately measured by the most sophisticated technological devices.

Scenes come into view, perhaps known, perhaps unknown to the dreamer. People, often strangers, get on stage, acting out incredulous, hilarious, fantastic, dangerous and confusing acts, and they say the wildest things, words that can be "heard," and many times have absolutely no meaning to the dreamer. Still, the dreamer slumbers on, unaware of what is next, as there is no one to announce what the scenes mean, or who the actors are. And there is color, perhaps vivid color, and symbols begin to emerge: a mirror, an old coffee pot, a dilapi-dated house, a dark closet, the list is endless as the dreamer strives to keep up with the images being impressed on the delicate stage of the dreamer's world.

Such is the mysterious world of the dreamer, a place humankind has chosen to visit over and over again since the beginning of time. No effort is needed from the dreamer to enter this nebulous world, no definite plan needs to be made, and the only surety is that once the hidden self begins to paint pictures, the dreamer will be guided, mysteriously by an invis-ible effort that orchestrates an incredible array of characters, scenes, fantastic worlds, plots, dialogue, encoded messages and at times horrific, frightening scenes that make the real world appear dull and bleak in comparison.

Then, the dreamer awakes and the images may disap-pear entirely or begin to play back vividly, at times fading away, as the dreamer struggles to capture what has been seen, heard, felt and experienced. If the dreamer is patient and not too quick to get off the bed to begin the daily routine of life, the images can be played once again, this time by the waking mind, haphazardly, as if juggling objects in the air. Some of the juggled images land, somehow, in the dreamer's memory nestling into the billions of electrical impulses already housed in the human brain, and there they wait for the dreamer to "see" them again and to venture back to the place where they were created to begin the process of uncovering their meaning. Some dreams may never be remembered, others will last in the dreamer's mind, perhaps for a lifetime. This "selection" of dreams to remember is often done unconsciously and perhaps with the consent of the dreamer who becomes aware that the dream has significance in the real world.

Capturing the Nebulous World

In this book, the dream world, along with the equally nebulous world of revelations, and visions will be explored at length with several goals in mind. First, what do revelations, visions and dreams mean for you? Secondly, what are you being asked to do, change, understand, or become? And finally, how do you make this invisible world work for you as a writer? By no means is this work set up to research scientific experiments on dreaming, or to collaborate with dream books that list symbols and their meanings. This is a personal look into the dynamic, intimate world that each carries within, a hidden world which, once identified, can be a source of great creative energy.

Dreams contain symbols of who you are. How you decipher the metaphorical language they contain is part of the lifelong process of learning the language of your own soul, which can also be defined as your spiritual being. In the real world, the more languages we speak, the greater career opportunities will be open to us, and the greater will be our ability to understand other cultures and customs. In the internal landscape of the soul, language must be learned individually, in a manner similar to that of a baby uttering words for the first time. Seeing things that may not make sense, we learn to observe, question, and finally connect symbolic meaning to current reference points in our lives, to our history, longings, fears, ambitions, and numerous other factors that define who we are.

At age twenty-three, I had a dream of myself entering an elevator. In real life, elevators are places I avoid if possible, as I have seen people get stuck in elevators, and wish to never have that experience. In this dream I entered the elevator with one desire in mind: to push the "down" button and get out of the building. Then a gentleman close by said very clearly to me: "This elevator only goes up." I had no choice, the doors closed, and I was on my way "up."

Even at that young age, I had already begun the process of getting acquainted with my internal landscape, which I did not formerly label as anything at all. I wrote the dream in my journal, and began to ask for its meaning. Later, I was to understand that I was indeed "trying to get out of doing something," which was to be a seminar leader at my local church for a group of women who were twice and three times my age. I had told the deacon that I simply could not lead these women as young as I was, and I recall that he gave a huge good-hearted laugh, and said, "Of course you can!" The man in my dream echoed the deacon's confidence by his words: "This elevator only goes up." I was being challenged to step up to the plate, and take on the task at hand. I did, and for reasons, still unknown to me, the women, some, indeed many years older than me, accepted me as a spiritual guide never once seeing my young age as a detriment to their learning.

The ability to devise meaning from an image in a dream will come only after the dreamer is aware of what the dream is referring to in real life, in the past, or in the future. But how does a dreamer connect the dots, and discover the personal messages hidden in the metaphors? Learning the language of your own soul is the key, as is awareness, love and faithfulness to self, and vigilance.

2

SPIRAL STAIRCASE: PROPHETIC DREAM

"It's right there, mija, what you have to do next.
It's right in front of you."

Francisco Moreno Duarte

IN April 1995, I had a dream. Not what I would consider a regular dream, but perhaps more correctly a vision within a dream. In the dream I was lost in a big building, and felt somewhat anxious as I searched for a room in which I was to present to a group of people. The building was so real I could actually hear water running through the pipes in the walls. I was unable to find the room where I was to present, and happened to see a stairway, leading down, which was where I wanted to go. I wanted out of that rather dreary place. Even in dreams, as mentioned, I avoid elevators, which are not my idea of reliable transportation. So, down I went, and at the bottom of the stairs I saw my father. There he was, or shall I say an image of him in his kaki pants, work shirt, hat and work boots, waiting for me. Without a word, he took my hand, and led me to an immense spiral staircase that climbed into the heavens. I saw it before me, salmon-colored, beautiful, and lost in the clouds and the dome of a perfectly blue sky. My father did not speak verbally, but I understood his message clearly. "It's right there, *mija*, what you have to do next. It's right in front of you." I was being addressed in the affectionate "*mija*," meaning "my daughter" in Spanish. The thought was as real to me as if my father had actually uttered the words out loud. Then, I awoke with the marvelous image of the spiral staircase in my mind.

Mysterious Message

Not seeing the end of something is a puzzling sensation. Where did it go—this elegant spiral staircase, lost in the clouds? What was I to do with such an image? The language of dreams comes to us in codes, images and symbols that may mean nothing in the natural world. Sounds, colors, and people, perhaps from the other world symbolize aspects of who we are, and show up in our dreams with no explanation. I came to realize that my internal world had chosen my father to deliver this life-changing message. I don't think I would have listened to anyone else. Seeing my father lead me to the spiral staircase got my attention, and his words had that much more meaning because my father was someone I loved and trusted. Later, I thought of my father having to grasp my hand in the dream, and lead me like a baby. It was a true image of where I was— lost in the everyday world, plagued by many problems, and unable to understand my purpose in life.

Yet, I had no idea what my father's words meant, nor what was "in front of me." There was nothing left to do, but to ask. And asking, as I have found, is a very humbling thing to do. Asking questions means we do not understand something; we may be confused or have lost our way. Often, we are so confused we do not know what "way" we have lost. Questions also are intersections, times when we stop to reflect about alternatives. If I go this way...I can expect these outcomes, if I go another way, a new set of outcomes will come into being. Over the years, I have learned how to allow myself to think in terms of extreme opposites in choosing my path. For instance in leaving a job, I think in terms of staying another year, and if it is a job that I no longer want, my internal person will rise up, and the "answer within" will be a huge, silent, NO! Then, I turn to the opposite and think what it would mean for me to leave the job, and if it is the right time to end the job, again my internal person will quickly "answer," YES! In between are gray areas, places where I may still have questions to ask, details I will need to work out, and possibly a waiting period, but the choice in either direction has been made.

My "Aha" Moment

For two weeks or more, I asked the dream for its meaning. I wrote in my journal, detailing the dream's description, and spun the details over and over again in my mind. What's in front of me? What is it I need to see? I argued with the dream, and with my father in the dream. There were lots of things in front of me, which one of those was I to *look* at? It seemed the more I asked, the less I understood. That is the formula for asking, which I had not yet learned. I would eventually come to the end of my questions, and in the process even the questions would be forgotten, then the answer would come, but at that time I felt helpless and no closer to the truth than when the dream had appeared.

One evening as I worked on research for university classes I was teaching, I decided to write out the dream on my computer. At that time, my writing space consisted of a narrow utility room lined with cabinets along both walls and a built-in desk. The walls were a bright turquoise, which made the room more attractive, but it was still a utility room, off the carport, housing the washer and dryer with no cooling or heating. In the summers I would set up fans to circulate the air and wear sleeveless blouses and denim shorts; in the winter I would set up a small heater and wrap myself in blankets or wear a sweater or jacket. I usually worked into the wee hours of the morning, and recall that it must have been about 1:00 a.m. in the morning when I decided to write down the dream on my computer.

As I wrote the words: "It's right there, *mija*, what you have to do next, It's right in front of you." I experienced what I would identify as an "aha" moment, a cathartic instant in time when a revelation rises into the conscious mind and becomes a reality, something you can actually see in front of you, hold in your hand so to speak. This new reality quickly took up what I *thought* was reality—the humdrum of my existence, working each day at a school district, besides tackling two other jobs teaching at a university and doing therapeutic counseling at a clinic, and all this, besides being a single Mom with four kids! There was little time for me to look to the internal for answers while living such a busy life. Yet, here was the spiral staircase, pointing upward, and the answer came like a thunderbolt. I remember saying the words aloud, "You mean I'm a writer?" It was as if every cell in my body responded with a resounding, "YES!"

Later, I was to understand that a truth had been revealed to me, a deep inkling that was greater than my formal use of language with its words, syllables, and sentences had led the way for me to understand my call to write. The dream had correctly prophesied what was to happen to me in the very near future. The image of my father, the spiral staircase, the sky overhead—all of it worked together to create *one* message. The way of the spirit is a holistic one, in which symbols add up to create one whole message. Unknown places in our internal beings appear that reach out to new possibilities, things perhaps never imagined.

Had someone told me that night, "Someday, your books will be published world-wide," I would have broken a rib laughing at such a fantasy. I had no intention of publishing, although writing and studying literature had always been my strong points. I was a no-nonsense person when it came to providing for my family. There were bills to be paid, food to be put on the table, and teaching was the career that provided the paycheck—end of story, or so I thought. The mysterious vision of the spiral staircase had "risen" to my conscious mind, and become a revelation, as visions often do. I was to write; that is what I had been born to do.

South African Mentor

The first rung of the spiral staircase was an important one. I had to learn to ask my internal being for answers. Then, I had to learn to trust that God would guide me in understanding the answers. Once on the first rung, huge doubts came to me. How was I to do this? What was I supposed to write? I knew absolutely no one who had actually published a book. Phoenix is not a city that fosters a vibrant literary community, yet the spiral staircase loomed overhead, and I had no idea how I was to climb it, nor what to expect once I started. This idea of *knowing* was to be something I would learn to give up. Knowing where I was going was not important; what was important was that I was on my way.

I wish I could say that my writing life began to bloom after the prophetic dream of my father, however, that is not what happened. The dream had only pointed the way, now the ball was in my court. To become reality, a prophecy needs the cooperation from the one who received the message. My father had not told me *what* I was to write, and that added to the confusion. It's funny how we begin to "argue" at times with the invisible. I found myself wanting an answer from my father, asking: "What, dad...what's in front of me? I don't understand." There were so many things in front of me; I felt the search would end before it even got started.

This struggle went on for weeks, until one night I decided to go to a nearby bookstore, and found myself walking up and down the aisles hoping to find something that would inspire me, and tell me what I was to write. I ran my hand across a bookshelf, and a book fell into my hands. As readers, we choose what we will read, and as a voracious reader I have read my share of Thomas Merton, C.S. Lewis, Annie Proulx, Charles Dickens, Mark Twain, Pearl Buck, Harper Lee, Isabel Allende, Garcia-Marquez, on and on, but on this particular night, the book chose me. It was a collection of short stories by Bessie Head, a South African writer who passed away in 1986. It wasn't until very recently that I discovered she died on April 17, 1986, and shared at least one similar date with my father; he was born on April 17.

The book, *Tales of Tenderness and Power*, depicted life in rural Africa. It attracted me for a couple of reasons. First, I very much enjoy reading stories from other countries, and second, the book was a slim size, and one that would not take a long time to read. I took it home and immediately began to read about the lives of villagers set in the landscape of rural Africa. I read about a couple who had fallen madly in love with each other despite their parents' outrage, and ran away to eventually share a mysterious union on a hill in Southern Botswana. There were tales of disputes between tribes over land and cattle, and stories of Anglos living among the Natives, clashing with traditional customs and beliefs. There were heart-wrenching episodes of love between Africans and Anglos—the underlying element of love waging war against prejudice and discrimination, similar to Bessie's own beginnings as a child born to an affluent English woman, and an African laborer. Bessie Head was born, a product of their illegal union in an insane asylum, which was the place her mother had been forced to go, once her pregnancy was discovered.

The cavalcade of wonderful characters Bessie Head depicted, so foreign from my own up-bringing, yet so close to my heart in the values they shared about family, tradition and the sanctity of freedom, all played a dynamic role in helping me understand one thing: *I was to write what I knew.* I also had a cosmos, a place where I had been raised, similar to Bessie Head's birthplace where people lived in a small town atmosphere, where life was slower and there was time to get to know one's neighbors. This was the kind of life I had experienced in the Sonorita Barrio in South Phoenix, a place that consisted of a maze of dirt roads and alleys forming a tapestry of pathways connecting humble homes that had little property value in the eyes of mainstream America.

The word *barrio* is not a Spanish word; it is an indigenous word from the Nahuatl language spoken by the ancient Mexicas of the Valley of Mexico, who would later be referred to as the Aztec Indians. They founded their imperial city of Tenochitlán in 1325, which the Spaniards described as one of the most splendid cities they had ever seen, on a marshland, indeed the city was a Venice of the New World. Eventually, the city would assume the name known to millions throughout the world: Mexico City. In more modern times, the word, Mexica, would come to indicate a Mexican-American, or a Chicano, a term referring to someone born on the American side of the border who had links with Mexico. The ancient term, *Xicanos*, (spelled with the 'x' used in Nahuatl) is an abbreviation of the word, Mexicas, and over the years the 'x' became the 'ch,' of the word—*Chicanos*.

My beginnings, not unlike Bessie Head's, were rooted in ancient rites, customs and myths, a mysterious world that made little distinction between the physical and the spiritual. It was a world that often stood in opposition to mainstream American values, seeming to be out-of-step with the social, political and economic landscape of America's materialistic search for happiness.

Brainstorming the Past

My next step was to allow an avalanche of memories involving people, places, events, and physical and spiritual dimensions of my life to surface. I began to brainstorm, that is, to let my mind freely explore my old *barrio* jotting down things as they came to mind without censoring anything or permitting my mind to hold back a memory. It was as if a dam had broken loose in my soul. I could barely write fast enough to capture the hundreds of memories, vivid, for the first time in years in my mind. The process was a sacred thing to do, as I was coming home to the real me, the person I had ignored for so long, thinking I had nothing to offer, nothing that anyone would be interested in. Unknown to me at the time, I had touched the creative energy within, and had released the writer, hidden in me since the day I was born. Creative energy, once released, is a formidable force. It defies all the normal constructs of thought and plunges into the heart of things. I became aware of my surroundings as never before, sensing through my mind, the sounds, smells, tastes, and feelings of where I had been, who had been with me, and what I remembered of conversations and memories that I thought had long been forgotten. I still have the pages of the original brainstorm I wrote, now worn sheets of paper with a jumble of scribbled words that make no sense to anyone else but me. Without realizing it, *I was learning the language of my own soul.*

Once a new image of myself began to rise, more questions came to mind. What was happening to me? Where was all this leading to? How could I manage my current life, and still search for something new? Life relentlessly went on. The sun came up, the moon rose at night, and in-between there were thousands of things to take care of: bills to pay, a hectic job to do at the school district, kids to get to school, a household to run, and two more jobs I worked at to support my family. And at night I wrote, and into the wee hours of the morning, heedless of the exhaustion I felt and the fact that I had to be at work by 7:00 a.m. Friends who knew my schedule would tease me, "You don't really have to sleep do you, Stella?" And I would smile, wearily, yet feel a sense of contentment as I knew I was finally living out who I was.

Awakening the Writer Within

I wrote two books, on a late-model Mac with a tiny square screen that vibrated a bluish glow. I often prayed as I opened a web page, as I never knew if my computer would have success in dialing an outside line and finding a web server, or not. Most times, the funny ringing tones ended in no server coming up. I watched my children as if from afar, they were so close, yet I had to separate from them in order to write. There was an invisible boundary that rose around me, and I was later to identify it as "the zone," a place that was owned by the writer within, something invisible had been created, yet it was very real. This "place" is known by all artists in one way or another, and also known is the pain of separation from one's work which becomes a type of crucifixion that haunts and puts despair into our daily lives.

I began to create, to give birth, and the labor I experienced was profound, not at all like having children, but one in which I felt a strange urgency; it was do or die. I was on a mandate to write. I sensed a deep desire to describe what I had seen and felt in my life. It was a pledge to myself that I would search out the pain and wonder of my life just as I had felt it and spin it into stories with brilliant threads that would form astonishing tapestries I could hang up like a series of movable paintings. What meaning the "paintings" would make was another mystery.

The Power of Prophetic Dreams

Prophetic dreams are unusual, dramatic, and often involve a vision, such as the spiral staircase that still lives on in my mind's eye. They are meant for the dreamer, and although they can prophecy world events, they generally do not. Their messages are usually meant for the dreamer, even if the dream involves scenes of the world and of other people. Words said to us as children can also carry great prophetic power, as often they form the basis for who we are. As we experience being loved, or unloved, accepted or rejected, punished unfairly or treated with respect, we begin to form a concept of the world: it is right or wrong, a good place to live in, or a place of pain and betrayal.

My father's prophetic words in the dream rushed into my life and within one year of the dream I had signed my first book contract for my short story collection, *Fragile Night*, (1997, Bilingual Review Press) centered on my own cosmos, the Sonorita Barrio in South Phoenix, as inspired by Bessie Head's tales. Five years later my first novel, *Let Their Spirits Dance*, (2002, HarperCollins) was bought for world rights by Diane Reverend of Cliff Street Books at HarperCollins, and bid on by eight of the top publishing houses in the U.S. Following fast on the heels of my first two publications came, *If I Die in Juárez*, (2008, University of Arizona Press) and *Women Who Live in Coffee Shops and Other Stories*, (2010, Arte Publico Press).

Over the years, many local awards have come my way, as well as awards with national recognition such as: the American Book Award, Women in American History Award, Independent Publisher's Book of the Year Award, Southwest Book of the Year Award, Foreword Magazine Book of the Year Award, the Barbara Deming Memorial Fund Award, Chicano/Latino Literary Prize, River City Writing Award, and a Pulitzer Prize nomination.

I created rituals, little ceremonies recognizing the work I was creating, and one of these was receiving the last pages of a finished manuscript from my printer on my knees, a symbol of humility before God for the honor of writing. In quiet, vacant churches, I would take my manuscripts bound with huge paper clips or rubber bands, and kneel at the altar, putting the manuscript in front of me, an offering to God, a grateful gesture for the gift of writing so graciously granted to me. It was also not uncommon for me to lay a manuscript by my side as I slept. During the night I would often put my hand over it, knowing that even in sleep, dreams can reveal important themes that belong to the manuscript. Our minds do not shut down in sleep; they remain active and filled with images that can inspire and powerfully affect our work.

As a prophecy unfolds, it seems the whole universe goes into action. A "red carpet" is laid out, and a whole new set of people and circumstances come into view. However, without the internal "yes," nothing else can be ignited. A person's "yes" or "no" determines if the prophecy will come true. Always, we have the ability to use free will to choose for, or against something that is being offered. The internal landscape within is an immense, sacred place, and presents symbols, images, words, and actions that may make no sense in the real world. I lost count of all the times I doubted myself. Was I truly on the right track? Were the risks I was taking, financially, personally, and emotionally what I was supposed to do? What if I was wrong, and had missed the meaning of the message entirely?

Yellow Pages to the Rescue

Once the prophetic energy engages in the soul, there is little that can stop it. One of the first things I wanted to do was connect with other writers, and did not know how to do this. I looked in the Yellow Pages of my local phone book, under "writers" and found Writer's Voice, an organization, now defunct, that had been established to create a community of writers. I contacted them, and found out they were offering a short story writing class with Melissa Pritchard, a well-established, award-winning author, and Professor of English at ASU. I signed up for the class, sending off a story I had written as an example of my work. Melissa accepted me, along with twelve other writers, and I began a semester-long class with her at a community center located in Tempe. Melissa was the first author to powerfully impact my work as a budding writer.

Although a lover of literature, I had yet to understand what the process of writing was all about. During my first peer critique in the class, I mistakenly thought that my first draft of a short story was the final, polished form! I had much to learn. Another surprise I experienced were comments made by my fellow writers saying things like, "You're a natural-born storyteller!" And, "I can't believe you haven't published anything." I was shocked by their reaction, as I felt I did not compare with some of the class members who had been writing for several years and had quite a bit of writing skill.

In similar fashion, as I started my novel, Writer's Voice was advertising a class with a man who would become a dear mentor, Ron Carlson. Again, I sent an example of my work, indeed a draft in a most elementary form, of *Let Their Spirits Dance*, and I was accepted to work with Ron Carlson, also a Professor of English at ASU. This dynamic writer was the first to help me understand how to construct a novel, how to "cut and paste," setting the scattered pieces of my narrative into a tight, seamless web.

I laughed at the comment he made one day, watching me take notes of everything he was saying: "Stella, I've never seen anybody work as hard as you do! Relax...eat more cookies!" I agree, writing should be fun as well, and have learned over the years how to stand back and laugh at life, at myself, and at the ironic, often nonsensical things that make up my "writer's mind."

From this first entrance into the writing world, one miraculous circumstance after another proved to me that not only was I being guided into the writing world, there was a "conscious effort" to help me every step of the way. There was more to my "yes" than I could have ever imagined. The prophetic message had begun to spin its own power in my life.

3

POSSIBILITIES: IDENTITY DREAM

You will be given a new identity.

CHANGING your image is a complicated thing to do. It is a photo developing, the details of its embossed picture, surprising you. Once I realized that change was taking over my life, it was all I could do to catch up with the consequences of the choices I was making. Several dreams came to my rescue, as did some experiences that I can only identify as "mystical."

One morning, almost a year after the prophetic dream of my father, I received a call from Arizona State University Bilingual Review Press informing me that, *Fragile Night,* had been accepted for publication. The night had been a troubling one for me with my younger daughter Deborah, at the time a teen, sick all night with a fever. I had been up with her most of the night, barely dozing off for a few moments of anxious sleep. Early in the morning as the sun was rising, I recall walking to my front door in a daze and as I peered eastward through a small window on the door's frame, I witnessed the brilliant orange rays of the rising sun illuminate the sky, and very softly, almost as if it was a secret between friends, a thought came to my mind: *You are rising too.* As tired as I was, I only glimpsed at the words in my mind, not realizing I had just received a revelation; another truth had been grasped by my conscious mind.

My attention instantly shifted to the task at hand. I was going to a pharmacy to pick up a prescription for my daughter. I walked to the utility room that posed as my office, and looked at the answering machine on my desk, the old-fashioned kind that blinked back a flashing red light when messages had been recorded. My first thought was to unplug it. I wanted no calls. I was staying home from work to tend to my daughter and the less I was disturbed, the better. I hesitated, and in a single instant, changed my mind, and left the machine on. Leaving my oldest daughter, Monica, in charge of Deborah and my younger son, John, I went to the pharmacy and upon returning noticed that the red light on the answering machine was flashing. I wondered, angrily, who had called me so early in the morning. I pressed the button, and heard: "This is Gary Keller from Bilingual Review Press. We're very impressed with your work, and would like to publish your collection of short stories. Call me at your earliest convenience."

The shock I sensed registered many times in my body, causing me to stand perfectly still with my mouth open. I pressed the recorder's button again and again, and again, each time incredulous. I had forgotten about my submission to Bilingual Review Press, as I had been busy submitting single stories to several publishers and contests that I had diligently located in the magazine, *Poets and Writers*, and in the latest version of *Writer's Market.* Dr. Gary Keller's voice penetrated the early morning silence over and over again with his message. My heart was racing as I realized that only minutes before I had been secretly told that I too, was rising, and here was the proof! All through that day, in-between tending to my daughter, I would race over to the answering machine, and play the message for my sisters, Rosie and Mary, and for friends, until they may have thought I had gone crazy, and still I could not believe the words, until I actually spoke to Dr. Keller, and he made an appointment for me to come in and see him and meet the staff and my editor.

It was a strange encounter as I walked into the publishing office at Arizona State University for the first time, and heard one of the staff members say: "The author's here." I actually turned around to see if an author had walked in through the door. I wondered who I would meet, perhaps one of the authors whose events I had attended. It would be my lucky day, as I had several favorite authors I longed to meet. It was the first time someone had identified me as an author, and the new identity was so new, I had no way of absorbing its meaning. Slightly embarrassed, I realized the staff member was talking about me.

Interpreting Human Nature

What was I to do about the beginnings of a whole new identity? How was I to incorporate the "new me" into the "old me," or would it be the other way around? My life seemed to be pressing forward at top speed, as family members stood by, some of them cheering for me, others in dismay, wondering what on earth I was thinking. Was I trying to be superior to them? Was I losing who I was? I was one of them, wasn't I? The Latino taboo against presumption, pride in self, and acting better than others, wove tangled threads in me, causing fear to settle in. At times, I felt I had to apologize for what I was doing...it was nothing I would explain, just a few stories, no, not about family members, exactly, except those whose names I had changed!

The gist of my work was places I had experienced such as, darkness, loneliness, loss, joy, love, sorrow, all universal themes that showed up in my characters. Later, I was to realize that, as an artist, I had been given the honor of "interpreting human nature." I often tell my creative writing students to be sure to change names if they write from memory to protect the guilty, the innocent need no protection.

Fragile Night went on to become a finalist for the Pen West Fiction Award, and I received a hand-written letter from one of the judges on the jury—Ursula K. Leguin. Her short letter astonished me: "Your stories reached my heart," she wrote. "You are one of the writers who will enlarge humanity. Keep writing." I held the letter in my hand, reading over and over again the message from this wonderful author who had been writing for over thirty years, before I had even put pen to paper, and tears of gratitude welled up. I *was* on the right track, here was an experienced author telling me that the magical dream of my father, the risks I had taken, the suspicion from family members, my own doubts—all of it was worth it. My dreams and visions were becoming reality. The realization of the writing mandate had begun.

Losing the Old for the New

More was brewing. I discovered that the energy of finding your identity is an urgent one. God, your own soul, the universe, angels, spiritual beings, dead writers, family and friends all play a part in what happens as you stand at a crossroads trying to decide which way to go. One of the things that helps you discover your way, and marks your life's important events, is keeping a journal. Since I was a young girl, I have had numerous journals, or diaries over the years. In the past fifteen years, I have also added dreams to my journals, and often mark them with post-it's, naming them: "Baby Dream," " Small Window Dream," "Old Shoes Dream," etc. This helps me to keep them, not only in my memory, but date them, and put them in the right time frame in my life. What is happening in real life at the time of a dream is often of up-most importance in understanding the dream's significance.

Also playing a vibrant role in uncovering the meaning of everyday occurrences, are revelations that crystallize in your mind as truths, and visions—images whose meaning are metaphors that must be seen as whole "instances," and whose significance is understood as a complete thought, the spiral staircase is a prime example of a vision within a dream. Visions play in our minds, at times, in bold images, at other times in blurred images that may seem to be only fleeting glances at a nebulous world. Our responsibility includes spending time in the internal landscape of self in silent prayer, meditation, or in whatever means we use to rid ourselves of the sensual, rushing world, and concentrate on the dark, silent world within which holds the secrets of who we truly are. Identity is realized as we become attentive to the internal world within.

Lost Purse Dream

Adding to my discovery of a new identity was a dream I had on November 7, 1999. In this dream I had lost my purse with all my ID. At first, I was afraid, then I came to terms with the fact that I would need new identification, a new driver's license, bank cards, etc. The message of the dream seemed to be: *you will be given a new identity.* Seven days later, the dream came true. I was at a grocery store, and lost, or had my ID stolen by someone when I placed it down on the counter as I wrote out a check for groceries. As in the dream, I was faced with no ID, and the fact that I had to get a new driver's license, besides calling the bank to tell them of my lost cards. The new identity that was coming was rushing in on me and once again, change was a given.

Change crept into many facets of my life, including my close, personal relationships in particular one I had cultivated for the past few months with a fellow writer, a man whom I had felt would be a good companion. We both felt we could combine our writing world while sharing the same cultural views, and family traditions. The risk would be minimal, wouldn't it? As time passed, I saw things that I could not endure: alcohol abuse, dependency, lack of motivation, and the man's inability to set parameters around his relationships with other women.

By this time, I had learned that change was something I had to do from *within*. I no longer wanted the role of the selfish make-over artist with the motto: "I'm going to change you if I have to die trying!" I took the opportunity to end the relationship after applying for a fellowship at Stanford University and using this as an excuse to move away from Phoenix with my younger son. If I received the fellowship, I explained, my son and I would move to California. The fellowship never materialized, yet it signaled the end of a relationship we had thought would last, with our love of writing as the common ground. As the years have passed, this decision proved to be the best for both of us, and we have remained friends.

More change loomed on the horizon. The revelation given to me as I watched the rising sun and experienced the loss of my ID in my dream and in real life, were intricately woven together. It is amazing to see how much of our internal world is *not* in our control! There was no way I could have ever orchestrated a rising sun, or the loss of my ID, or the call from Dr. Keller. I have found that once a truth is revealed, it begins to infuse new energy into our real lives and the change we thought we would contend with takes on new dimensions and we are faced with change building on change; a path is cleared, and new paths are created. It can also be a time of great uncertainty as we do not know exactly what the new identity will be. Risk is always a part of accepting the unknown, and at this particular time in my life, I knew something new was just around the corner; I had no idea how close it was.

4

OUT OF DARKNESS: RECURRING DREAM

*If you come to terms with the dark parts of who you are,
you won't have to marry them.*

Darkness is a teacher. As we mince our way through
life's demanding routines, tragedies and joys, there is little
time to reflect on our journey or to make sense of what is in
front of us. It's easy to turn away from challenges and enter
a time of internal darkness where no answers come, no new
visions develop, and the soul seems to be asleep. No one wants
to cultivate darkness, yet there are times when a dark time will
finally reveal the truth.

One story that caused me to take a closer look at the concept of darkness as a teacher was my mother, Rosanna Pope's,
account of a vision she experienced one dark night in the alley
next to our home. I do not recall when this incident happened,
and in fact, it may have occurred before my birth, however, as
a child, I remember my mother telling of her experience many
times. Each time, her eyes would glow with the passion of her
words, and whether the listener believed what had happened
to her or not, one could see that *something* had happened.

43

Here is her story as accurately as I can recall it.

One night I went out to throw some trash in the alley. The night was so dark, I could barely see my hand in front of my eyes. I walked slowly down the alley, and got to the place where we left our trash, and after I had put the bags in the garbage can, I saw a bright light, muy brillosa, very brilliant, so beautiful, but it didn't hurt my eyes. I was so surprised to see this light, I can tell you, oh, and you may not believe what happened next, but you must...I saw Christ, hanging just like he hangs on his cross, on the telephone pole that was before me. I saw him so clear, the nails in his hands and feet, his side pierced, and the crown of thorns, so clear, I could not take my eyes off of him. What a beautiful sight, so holy! I walked backwards slowly down the alley, because I didn't want to take my eyes off "mi Cristo." I got to the kitchen door, and I said, "Let me call my husband." Then I rushed in and your father was sitting at the kitchen table drinking coffee. "Come out, Chico, and see!" I shouted, "Christ in the alley!" But by the time your father came out, the alley was dark again, and Christ was gone.

Some may ask if my mother really did have a vision of Christ in that dark alley so long ago, and no one will ever know for sure. Story is profound, it searches us, changes us, challenges us, and that is what this story did in my mother's life. She told the story with passion and conviction...something had happened to her. Many years after her vision in the dark alley, my mother lay dying in my home. Now she was eighty-four years old, suffering, weak, and near death. She had told me, "I want to go to your house. I want to die with you." This was indeed an honor for me, as I had also been directed from within while saying my prayers to "Go get your mother." Two weeks before her death my mother related seeing the light again...the same light she had seen in the dark alley as a young mom.

"I'm seeing the light again."

"What light," I asked.

"The same one I saw in the alley, remember? It's very bright," she said, "but it doesn't hurt my eyes." Then she connected the puzzle pieces. "Oh, now I know why they say that God is the Light of the World...He is! And this light has love for each and every person, "*cada persona,*" were her words in Spanish. The light she had seen as a young mom had searched my mother out again, like a laser beam, finding her at the end of her life on her death-bed and comforting her, strengthening her for her final journey.

After Any Dark Time in Your Life

Story is revealed in layers. As a very quiet and introverted child, my mother's story empowered me in an inexplicable manner, not obvious in my outward behavior, but deeply rooted in my psychic. I did not know any other girl whose mother had seen Jesus Christ on the cross in a dark alley...so there! The beauty of Mom's story took hold in my life, as did her attachment to the dream world and to interpreting her own dreams aloud, as I listened intently, analyzing the images in my own child's mind. Without realizing it, Mom was giving me the "mind of a writer," the art I would need to penetrate dark times, interpret them for meaning, and create characters who would evolve in spite of their pain.

In the eyes of mainstream America, my beautiful, half-Irish Mom, the daughter of Solomon Pope, her blue-eyed, Irish Dad, and Claudia Rivas his *mestizo* wife, was an uneducated Mexican woman who had not even completed elementary school. The only job I ever recall her having outside the home, was working at a nearby laundry. Her artistic nature, however, was not diminished, as her internal world was rich with meaning, and she learned how to connect words to visions and decipher obscure messages. Her own "Irish melancholia" would at times get the best of her over the years, most of it related to bitter memories of Dad's drinking lived out in the earlier part of their marriage. As time passed she began living a reclusive life, praying and meditating, especially on Christmas Eve when she would spend hours in prayer before the Christ Child, instead of celebrating with her huge, noisy family.

As painfully shy as I was in school and in other social settings, at home, my ideas were unleashed and I often had the neighborhood kids perform dramas of the stories I had read at Harmon Park Library which was close to our family home. I would promise the "little urchins," nieces, nephews and neighbors, a cupcake, candy, a nickel, whatever it took to get them to perform the stories I could see like videos inside my head. My brain worked like a camera, and this I see as a strong point in children and adults who have "photographic memories." I was able to describe in detail what I saw, long after the event or "scene" was over. It never occurred to me to tell anyone, nor did anyone ask me what I was thinking, they simply said, "Stella likes to tell stories to the kids." Love of reading, fosters love of storytelling and writing. Never underestimate the power of a child who loves to read—truly, they hold the world in their hands!

At times I would walk several miles to downtown Phoenix to spend time reading at the Phoenix Public Library on Central Avenue, the biggest branch open in Arizona. A child alone in a world of books, I felt I had floated up into Heaven! Reading about the saints and their glorious lives of sacrifice and love for God worked a special commitment in me. I decided for a while, that I too, wanted to be a martyr and die for the love of God. I read of saints burned at the stake, pulled on racks, spit upon and tormented in so many ways by a "pagan" world, and I resolved to try to make up for all this abuse by being, "holy." I prayed on my knees at all hours of the night, often spooking my little sister, Lupe, who would wake up in the middle of the night, and find me praying before a religious picture in our room. Secretly, I would "hold my breath," for seconds at a time, thinking I was offering a sacrifice to God as the saints had done. Since God had given me the breath of life, I figured I would offer it back to Him as a gift. I even considered joining a convent as a young woman, and was often referred to as *la monja*, the nun.

All this was part of the secret life I lived as a child, which I have never disclosed before, until this moment. It never occurred to me to tell anyone what I was thinking, and in a large, busy family no one ever questioned me—I was left to my own devices. Now, I look at children inundated with media, movies, television, cell phones, on and on, and I wonder if they still have a secret life going on within where they can rest, explore and reflect on the wonders of life. Solitude is at a premium in our world, and it is short-changing the development of the huge internal world that children naturally want to connect to. Addictions of all kinds often arise when a person is fragmented and cannot find wholeness; they will find a sublime experience, *even if it is fabricated by a drug.*

Like Mom, I was attracted to telling stories, and thinking about characters and scenes, while searching for the story's deeper meaning. It was all I could do to contain the words dancing in my head as I read fairy tales, adventure stories, biographies—everything seemed to "speak to me." As a Freshman in high school, I began to collect words, determined to learn as many new ones as I could. I spun the words around, reflecting on their meaning and sound, using them in sentences and poetry to release me from another kind of darkness, similar to Mom's—a darkness that would engulf me for the greater part of my life: depression. When the dark cloud of foreboding and melancholia would strike, fear would set in, as I had no idea how deep the darkness within would go, nor when it would release me.

During these times, I had trouble concentrating, and felt a deep sadness that gripped me and froze every joyous feeling I had ever experienced. Little by little, the darkness within would fade away like a dark cloud of pollution disappearing in the distance, and I would return to the edges of light once again. As an adult, my mother's story seared me, searched me, and taught me one of the most profound lessons of my life. It is this: *After any dark time in your life, there will be light, splendid light, and you will understand why you had to walk the darkness.*

At the end of her life, the light came once again to prove to my mother God's ever present spirit. This is what is identified as the *arc of the story*—what happens at the beginning of the story, swings like a huge arc, and is reflected at the end of the story. Light, the kind that crystallizes awareness and brings interior knowledge, love and peace penetrates the darkness, and releases us from our own fears. Without the darkness, light would only be an illusion. Over the years I have learned to say this prayer: "Lord, don't alleviate me, until you illuminate me." This is one of the most risky prayers I have ever uttered. Its challenge is that I will endure whatever is happening to me, either physically or spiritually, and not seek relief, until I understand what the darkness was sent to teach me for the good of my soul. My mother's vision in the dark alley inspired me over the years to contemplate the role of darkness in my life and develop stories that would search out the darkness within my characters as well.

The Masks We Wear

Darkness was my theme in *Fragile Night*, as my characters identified their masks, and saw their own distorted reflections in the mirror of self. We all wear masks which comprise different faces we exhibit in a given day, and it is up to each of us to identify the masks we wear and the personalities that go along with them. Loss of identity can come when we begin to believe we *are* the masks we are wearing without looking further into the layers of self and identifying the real person, the real, I am, within.

For instance, if a person can see the part of self that is angry, and know that this part could cause havoc, even death to another, the possibility of this happening will be greatly diminished by the mere fact, that now, the person knows the anger is there and can do something to bring this emotion under the control of the internal will. Not being aware that anger exists within could mean the unleashing of emotions that would inflict pain on the self and others. Emotions are the earth's daily roller-coaster ride. It is up to each of us to dominate our emotions, run ahead of them as if running ahead of a group of children about to cross a busy street. Emotions will go as far and as wide as they are allowed to go, yet once acknowledged, they can be used to bring about healing and to create a safe expression for feelings.

The words that open *Fragile Night*, invite the weary traveler to be patient as, "darkness in the end will reveal the light." These words instantly give the reader the parameters for the collection. The stories confront universal themes of darkness, and the mystery of saying "yes" when we mean "no." Characters come to their own "aha" or in Spanish "*ijuela*," experiences, sometimes humorously so, sometimes in a very dramatic and vivid manner that offers them a chance to recoup who they are and recreate themselves anew. Characters will confront their worst nightmares and some will learn how to sit in the darkness, allowing their own souls to speak to them, as my protagonist, Alma, does in the main story, "Fragile Night."

Learning to Examine Your Own Heart

Alma sits in the dark with a rosary tangled through her fingers, recalling the words of her grandmother, Abuelita Minerva, who insisted that Alma did not love her husband, Alfredo. Alma angrily rushed to defend herself by saying that she had his children, only to be told by her grandmother that the children had nothing to do with real love. Years of marriage, and her husband's alcoholism and involvement with the sexy and "loose woman," Cecilia, only heightened Alma's pain, and finally, the dream world came to her rescue in one of the most powerful ways imaginable: a recurring dream.

Often, if we refuse to come to terms with our own darkness, our dreams will hasten to our aid, replaying for us the same theme over and over again, until we are ready to understand what we must do. Alma was the young woman I had been who suffered in a violent marriage. My grandmother was not as prominent in my life as in Alma's, however, the message of Alma's recurring dream was truly my own. A recurring dream comes in a very purposeful manner to attract our attention. Its message is repeated many times, because once understood, the dream has the capacity to change the dreamer's life; yet the dreamer must be ready for the change.

The recurring dream I describe in the story came to me over a span of twelve years and always had the same theme. I would see my ex-husband going off with a "lady of the night," a prostitute, sleazy, in sexy clothes, her lips and nails painted bright red. In the dream I would call out to him, "She doesn't love you, don't you understand? You're so dumb, she doesn't love you!" Then I would wake up and review the dream as another message of my ex-husband's betrayals. But, it went further than that. The dream revealed only in part, my ex-husband's unfaithfulness, however, as most dreams are meant for the dreamer, the greater part of the message was for me.

The dream probed me, searching the very core of who I was for the truth. No one had betrayed me before I had *first* betrayed myself, lying to myself about why I stayed in the marriage. In the story, Alma, as I did, discovered, after sitting in the dark for many nights, that she herself was the "prostitute" in her dreams. Her grandmother had been right all along; she had never loved Alfredo. She had thought that having his children was proof of love, and had never stopped to do one simple thing: *examine her own heart.*

Examining your own heart is one way of being honest about your choices. It is a way to learn to choose what's good for you. It amazes me when I find myself making wrong choices, and *continuing* in the same direction, in spite of obvious consequences. Often, we want from someone else what we ourselves should be doing. In my long years of counseling, I have often heard clients talk about needing an "honest person," or "someone who truly loves them," without for one moment contemplating that they have never been honest with themselves, nor have they cultivated any love for self. Yet, they want someone else to come and do for them what they should first do for themselves.

Alma discovers, as I did, that the "whore," she saw over and over again in her dreams was a reflection of how she had "prostituted," herself in the marriage—living with a man she did not love. Over the years, my recurring dream would change slightly, but the theme was always the same. One day, as I washed dishes at my kitchen sink, the revelation of the dream rose to my conscious mind. This was several years before the prophetic dream of my dad and the spiral staircase. I could have never imagined that the dream would play a prominent role in something I would write and publish, much less that this experience would be the central theme of a collection of stories.

When a truth is revealed about the meaning of a dream as important as this one, we will often remember clearly where we were, who was with us, and even details about the weather, what was playing on the radio, on and on. I recall the exact address of our house in Phoenix at the time, even though we had lived in over 25 locations. Standing at the kitchen sink, I could hear my two-and-a-half year old son, John, and my eight year-old daughter, Deborah, playing with toys in the living room. My two older children, teens at that time—Vincent and Monica were not at home.

Suddenly, to my conscious mind rose these words: *You're the prostitute*. To say the least, I was shocked! Quickly, I began to defend myself from the harsh words. "I teach religion classes! I play music and sing every Sunday at church...I am absolutely NOT a prostitute!" But the words "lay quietly in my mind," as simply as if they had been put there by an unseen hand. No audible voice was heard, and in fact, had I heard something, I would have been frightened, as this is not the way I receive messages. The revelation continued: *Oh, yes you are because you're with a man you don't love. You're worse, a prostitute at least gets money—you get NOTHING!*

I recall being overwhelmed by the accusation, and holding onto the edge of the sink, feeling as if I would fall to the floor. The words were raw, signaling disorder within, shame, dishonesty, and lack of self-love. Yet, I knew they were the truth, and truth, once grasped has the capacity to set into motion instantaneous change. And that is what happened.

Darkness is a teacher. It strips us of all that is false, and in its emptiness, we search the deepest parts of self and find out where we have been wrong. This was difficult for me. I was a proud, young woman who felt I had power over my ex-husband. He would change; he would see things my way because my way was the right way. He was in the wrong, and I was in the right. All around me, my friends and family fed into the image I held of a suffering woman who loved her children and wanted to keep her marriage.

It would be years and years of heartache and wallowing in "pity parties," where I would symbolically sit for hours contemplating how unjustly my ex-husband treated me, and how I did not deserve this treatment, before I would learn that I was the "bad guy," too. Why? Because, I was trying to change someone who didn't want to be changed. I was trying to force my ex-husband to stop drinking and to be the good husband, father and leader of the family, while the whole time I was relishing in the fact that he couldn't do it, and next to him I was so much more intelligent, wiser and worthy of something better. I had never honestly examined my own heart with the question: "Do I love him?"

Our marriage had been done in haste, I was expecting our first child, and still wanted to please God and obey the sanctions of the Church, no matter what. I felt I must marry him as my sin, in my own eyes was too great. I sought punishment. In fact, I was a self-abuser, a person who bitterly criticized myself, who found fault with almost everything I did. Nothing was right about me. I had dropped out of the university and forfeited all my plans. I was a disappointment. Positive confirmations from family members were often, simply not there, and my own sense of self spiraled downward, until there was little self-esteem left. Not understanding the motives of my own heart, I did not know that I sought an abuser, someone who would continue the mistreatment I had begun on a grander scale—he was a reflection of who I was!

Awareness: The Next Step Upward

We were a perfect fit. Together, my ex-husband and I fed the darkest parts of who we were. I kept his image going as the "Black Sheep of the Family," and he kept my image as, "Ms. Goody Two-Shoes." I now know the antidote for this internal disease: *If you come to terms with the dark parts of who you are, you won't have to marry them.* What I did not want to correct within myself, I sought to control in my ex-husband. Instead of coming to terms with my own anger, revenge, violence, jealousy and so on, I wanted to control those things in him. I was a one-woman circus ring-leader, but I had the wrong person in the ring! Once I discovered that my "dark times" were often brought on by my own choices, I was able to end the "pity parties," and in fact got so strong, that when I saw a "pity party" beginning, I would literally hold up my hand and say, "I'm done with that. The pity parties are over!"

Awareness is a key that opens the door for great creative power. As long as I was unaware of my own selfish needs, I was unable to do anything about them. When I turned my "eye" within, I was able to see that the things I disliked most in my ex-husband were things that were often a part of who I was. This is where a choice was presented. I could walk up or *down* the spiral staircase. The "yes" that had initially sparked my journey up the spiral staircase could turn into a "no," by simply refusing to honestly deal with my own internal world. There is always a choice, no one is cast into a mold, unless the person is a child at the mercy of cruel caregivers or an adult who has no control over an abuser, otherwise the decision to grow is a personal one and provides for the exercise of free will. We are responsible for our own freedom, our own growth as human beings, and every decision we will ever make reflects our personal choices.

Lessons Learned from the "Boogey-Woman"

The Weeping Woman, alias La Llorona of Mexican folklore, also came out of the darkness in *Fragile Night* in the first story, "What La Llorona Knew," to teach me another aspect of darkness. I felt a strange sensation when I realized this villainous, ghostly character wanted my attention. She had been our official *boogey-woman*, the one we dreaded to meet on some dark night as she searched for her children, or so we were told. It took me a while to "sit down within" and look at her.

There is something about a grieving person that makes us uncomfortable, makes us want to turn our faces away, or tell the person not to cry, "It will be alright, life goes on," we might say, patronizing, hoping the grieving person will go away. In this instance, she would *not* go away, and I found myself reaching out to her, wanting her to tell me her story.

Darkness can endure our secrets, our failings and our heartaches in a huge dark pool that seems to be infinite. Legend tells us that La Llorona whose real name may have been Maria, was once a beautiful woman who would pay the penalty for considering herself better than others and anticipating that her beauty would hold the man of her dreams. She violated the Latino taboo, which warns against being presumptuous and conceited. She had a rude awakening when her husband, Gregorio, ran off with another beautiful woman, just as everyone had warned her he would do. Ambushed by her own pain, after seeing Gregorio with the other woman, Maria drowned their two children in a nearby river as she realized her husband loved the children and did not love her anymore. Instantly, as she saw the children's bodies carried off by the waves, she wanted them back, and began running wildly up and down the riverbank, heedless of rocks and the thick roots of trees, reaching into the water, trying to save the children from drowning. Finally, she fell against a huge stone, ending her own life. The next day, her parents discovered her body, and the whole town realized what she had done. The priest, did not allow her body to be brought into the town, and instructed her parents to bury her out by the riverbank. It was then that she transformed into the ghostly figure that frightened us as children, and one who would permeate Latino literature, history and folklore for centuries to come.

According to legend, she cries nightly for her children searching for them in every human face she sees. Her cry is a hideous wail that sends shivers up and down the backs of anyone foolish enough to be out late at night.

A Timely Message

In "What La Llorona Knew," Elena's mother, who lived in her daughter's home, shared her own Llorona story with her daughter one evening after Elena argued with her husband over her mother's nightmares and nocturnal walks. On the night in question, Elena caught up to her mother, and for the first time in her life decided to walk with her, setting the stage for two crucial elements of storytelling: someone has to be ready to tell the story, and someone has to be ready to listen. That night the two elements merged into one, and Elena learned her mother's secret.

Walking out into the backyard, with stars shining overhead, Elena's mother began the story of her sufferings as a young girl, and of a certain captain during the Mexican Revolution who had raped her as his troops had invaded her father's ranch. Eventually, she delivered the captain's baby, a boy, only to have the child cruelly taken from her and given to the captain's wife. It was then that her nightmares had begun, as her yearning for her son became a fire within that would not be quenched.

The darkness, once shielding La Llorona's own grief, rose over Elena and her mother in the story, and the lesson learned was a memorable one. Elena's mother explained to her daughter that only the night could endure La Llorona's pain. The darkness afflicted La Llorona by reviving her pain, yet it cradled her in its huge black fingers until she was soothed, and most importantly: it bore her wounds. Elena's mother understood the intimate connection between *darkness and pain*.

The story of La Llorona as told by two modern women reveals to us many truths. Darkness harbors our worst fears and our deadliest secrets; it is a force that can endure humankind's wickedness. Valiantly, La Llorona still searches the darkness for the parts of herself she chose to destroy. The parts of herself that looked most like her, she chose to destroy, and now she wants them back. This is an honorable desire, to undo the wrong we have committed and make it right again. Yet, her sorrow brings us horror and we flee from her as darkness and despair bring to life her heinous crime.

There is one thing that would have proven fatal to the darkness of La Llorona, and that would have been integrity and the cultivating of self-love. If La Llorona (Maria) had learned to love and respect herself, none of this would have happened in the first place. She would have had the sense to know that her life could go on without Gregorio, but instead, her own sense of identity had been masked by her need to be approved in the eyes of a man, instead of in her own eyes. The first betrayal she experienced, was self-inflicted. She was the first to be untrue to herself—a lesson I understood only too well.

The Generous Universe

Darkness has the capacity to disarm us, strip us of all contention, wound us, and yet hold us close. Darkness baffles me when I have found myself choosing wrong over right. At times, knowing something was not good for me, with eyes wide open to danger, I still chose darkness over light---another mystery of good vs. evil. This is portrayed by the character in my story, "Penguin's Mother," in some ways another auto-biographical story of *Fragile Night*, reflecting an even darker time in my life. It seemed I had understood the lessons about needing to love myself, to gain a true appreciation of who I was, and stop the terrible life-long habit of criticizing myself for every infraction under the sun, yet I had not learned how to *remember* the lesson in my daily life. I still had to practice the lesson over and over again!

The universe is very generous. If we have not learned that the choice we made was deadly, another occasion will come up with another choice and we will be given another chance to choose, which is one of the main reasons we are on this earth: *to learn to choose what's good for us.* It's the story of Adam and Eve each and every day lived out at many levels in our lives. I cringe within when I think of how many times this ancient story of creation has been used to batter women and blame them for introducing evil into the world, (the serpent) when in fact, it is a metaphorical story with many profound meanings, one being that somewhere along the line humankind chose *away* from God. Humans selected a selfish, self-centered existence, instead of a life centered in God.

The internal world poses a question: Do you want to choose destructive thoughts and actions rooted in bitterness and anger, or cultivate thoughts of forgiveness and love? Light vs. darkness, good vs. evil are universal themes played out in almost every story written in the history of humankind. It reminds me of a reflection about two wolves written anonymously by a Native American poet.

A Native American grandfather was talking to his grandson about how he felt. He said, "I feel as if I have two wolves fighting in my heart. One wolf is the vengeful, angry, violent one. The other wolf is the loving, compassionate one." The grandson asked him, "Which wolf will win the fight in your heart?" The grandfather answered, "The one I feed."

In this poignant rendition of good vs. evil, the decision for becoming a "greater human being," rests solely on the individual person. Taking responsibility in my own life, meant deciphering the meaning of the recurring dream that had over the course of twelve years related the same message: *I did not love the man I had married.* I had entrapped myself in a marriage that I knew had been wrong from the very start. Armed with the ultimatum that I would not go on another "roller coaster ride," brought on by his drinking, I faced my ex-husband the same day the dream's meaning was revealed to me, and told him: "You will never be my husband again!" He laughed at the words, as we had endured seventeen years of an off and on relationship beset by domestic violence and many separations. I remember he stood by silently watching the children and me before he left. That very day, although plagued with doubts and great fears about splitting up my family, my words sealed the end of our relationship.

After my divorce, I began the long journey of learning how to be true to myself. I began to experience love and respect for myself as beautifully reflected in one of the 20th century's most prolific Christian writers, Thomas Merton, "If my heart does not first belong to me, how can I give it to another?" Merton sheds light on one of the first requirements for understanding the power of love and choice: *love starts within or it doesn't start at all.* You cannot hope to truly love another, until you have learned to love and esteem yourself. Christ's words ring true: "You shall love your neighbor as yourself." (Matthew 19:19)

Having understood so much, at this point, I did not realize that just ahead lay a rude awakening. The process of learning something new must end in transformation, and the cultivating of a new self, or the lesson will be repeated all over again—compliments of the *generous universe.*

From the Frying Pan Into the Fire

The story "Penguin's Mother," not one of the original stories of *Fragile Night*, came about after all the other fourteen stories had been written, and I submitted it for the collection just before publication of the book. By this time, I had experienced another wrong choice that almost cost me my life. As the saying goes, I went from the "frying pan into the fire."

Through my sister Rosie's prison ministry, I had become acquainted in 1992 with a man in prison, and had begun writing to him, although at first, with great fear. The fear should have been my parameter, it was meant to signal a warning, which I did not heed. Danny, (an alias name) became prominent in my life through a series of letters, phone calls, and visits to see him at various prison facilities over a span of four years. Ignoring advise from those who had dealt with inmates, including ministers who tried to "talk some sense into me," I went headlong into a relationship that ended up entangling me with the most destructive person I would ever bring into my life, and into the lives of my children.

My measuring rod was that he claimed to be a born-again Christian, and he was active in playing Christian music and seeking a life in Christ. I have always been the kind of person who likes to give second-chances, my masters degree in counseling has led me to work with people over the years who have experienced huge changes in their lives, and in my own distorted mind I thought this would be the case. I look back, and think of the enormous risks I took with my life and the lives of my precious family members, friends and community, and shrink back in horror realizing how close I was to losing my life on occasions when this man threatened me with death. If I have ever seen a sociopath close up, it was in this instance. The relationship ended in his coming out of prison and "marrying me," although I was later to find out the marriage was illegal because he was already married. Not even a year into the marriage, I had already filed for an annulment.

Within a week of his coming out of prison, we had already experienced a break-up. The so-called marriage would last only a few months, although those months were filled with separations, his abuse of drugs, domestic violence, theft by him of all monies in my accounts, the filing of bankruptcy, my loss of self-love and confidence, and calls made to police, so many, I lost count. The final act was his theft of my son's social security number. John, then only eight years old, according to police records had committed felonies including theft, drunk driving, and drug charges. When my son turned fifteen and sought to get his driver's permit, I went to local detectives and worked with them, bringing evidence that would cause them to expunge all traces of wrong-doing from my son's life as they investigated evidence tracing Danny to all the criminal activity.

Anonymous Protagonist

From this darkest of times, came a sliver of light, the awakening that I had to come to terms with the dark parts of who I was *once again*, regain my own sense of love for self, and choose what was good for me all over again. To help me do this came a powerful, wise woman in the form of my protagonist in "Penguin's Mother." She is the only protagonist who did not give me a name. Instead, she offered herself as a nameless reflection of my own darkness, opening the way for a remarkable healing.

In the story she was a beautiful, young woman who had suffered the betrayal of her husband. She lived in the Projects in Phoenix with her two children in a tiny, run-down apartment with only the bare essentials for furniture and snoopy neighbors who wanted to know everything about her life, reminiscent of the many tattered apartments I had lived in with my own children.

One day she was faced with one of her ex-husband's cousins, a man straight out of prison named Marco. In this one story, I took the liberty of using an actual name, although Danny had used numerous aliases, his real name was Marco. In the story, the woman's son, nicknamed, Penguin, was a first grader who suffered a leg deformity that made him walk like a penguin, thus the nickname. His sister, Katrina was in junior high, and both were soon to meet Marco. The story dealt with the sexual abuse of a child, and although this did not happen with my children, the darkness makes no distinction, abuse is abuse, and all forms are deadly.

Penguin's mother worked at a local slaughter house at night where she saw animals butchered every day, and helped to cut up meat that was then packaged for sale. Each night she returned from work in the wee hours of the morning after her shift was over and picked up her children from her neighbor's apartment. Her work setting was to collide in the story, tragically, with her real life in a single instant when she faced the greatest antagonist of her life, whom she herself had brought into her home, also reminiscent of my own wrong choice.

One morning, after walking her children to the school bus stop, Penguin's mother found herself alone in her apartment. It was the day before Thanksgiving, and she was busy mopping and cleaning up, when there was a knock at her front door. When she asked who it was, she heard a man's voice on the other side of the door. At first, she thought it was the voice of her ex-husband, Roberto, and only opened the door after she heard the man claim he was, Marco, her ex-husband's cousin. Penguin's mother opened the door and saw a duplicate of her ex-husband: a man with wavy, dark hair, moustache and crinkly brown eyes. He appeared friendly and solicitous.

Instantly, Marco began to take inventory of his cousin's beautiful ex-wife, and began his plan on how to collect from Roberto, for all the mishaps they had lived out as cousins. Disarming Penguin's mother with his charm and good looks, he slowly won her confidence, although she remained wary, and eventually he found his way into her bed. Initially, she was horrified by her lack of Christian morals as this had been one of her greatest strengths and she sought to throw him out with no success.

Murder in the Dark

Ingratiating himself with the children, who were thrilled to have a man pay attention to them, Marco stayed day after day, and Penguin's mother was helpless to drive him out, until she noticed bruises on her small son's fragile body, indicating sexual abuse. It was then she realized what Marco had been doing, and her plot of revenge challenged me to write my first murder scene. So engrossing was her darkness that Penguin's mother no longer attended church, and met with Marco only in the dark. On the night she executed his murder she sent her children away to be taken care of by Esperanza, her neighbor. Then she set up the apartment like a huge darkened stage, turning off all the lights, except for one candle with a picture of the Sacred Heart of Jesus glowing on the bureau in her bedroom.

Marco arrived at the apartment, drunk, and stumbled in as Penguin's mother called him from her bedroom. He cursed the darkness, and mocked her under his breath, claiming that she was like all the rest—all she wanted was sex. He found her sitting in the middle of the bed, dressed in an old robe, her legs crossed. She looked like a Buddha, sitting so still in the candle's dim light, and he thought she was ready to play a game with him. He advanced, playfully reaching for the buttons on her robe, and telling her how much he loved to play games. Penguin's mother, through clenched teeth, told him she was sure he loved games, very sure, especially with little boys! Marco raised his hand to slap her, but was stopped cold by her quick action as she took out a butcher knife and sunk it deep into his throat.

The heinous act committed, Penguin's mother took a shower, washed off the knife, then snuffed out the candle of the Sacred Heart of Jesus, the light's glow reflecting her tears. She walked back to Esperanza's apartment and told her to call the cops as there was a dead animal in her bedroom. Later, she was arrested and taken to the police station where she spent the night laughing, crying and shaking at the same time, until she felt she had let go of all the trapped, ugly feelings of her life. Eventually, a judge declared her "insane" when she committed the act, and she was released from prison.

To say the least, I was shocked at the turn of events in this, the darkest story, of the collection, yet I felt I had to include it, as it illustrated how chaotically one can become when overtaken by darkness, and in spite of it all, once all the trapped, ugly feelings are dealt with, light can be regained once again. Light can always surface, no matter how penetrating the darkness becomes.

In counseling victims of sexual abuse, I try to make them aware that even though their physical body has been assaulted and violated, their spirit remains intact. No human hand can touch the spirit—it is God's sacred ground. A person's spirit may be crushed for a time, may sense great oppression, almost fade away, yet it is still there, a guarantee of God's love and faithfulness.

❧

Darkness is a teacher. If we look into the dark parts of our own lives, we will encounter the truth, explore our dreams, come to terms with our ghosts, and we will see parts of ourselves alive and well in the darkness, and they will live on in the characters we create. Healing for self and others can come through stories told from the heart, stories that reflect the human condition and inspire readers to reach for the light no matter how dark the darkness becomes. In the end, light will come to make all things new again.

5

REVELATION: PASSION FLOWER

It's the passion flower your mom
had when you were a kid.

As a historical novelist, I have spent hundreds perhaps thousands of hours, researching into the history, culture and perspectives of my stories in order to accurately create the background and conflicts my characters will face. This was the case in writing my first novel *Let Their Spirits Dance*. In 1998, I visited Ho Chi Minh City, founded in 1698, also known as Saigon, with a small group of Americans to complete research, which included conducting interviews, and visiting sites important to combat soldiers during the war. The novel tells the story of a Chicano/Latino family from Arizona living in post-war Vietnam. Chicano, as mentioned, is derived from the word *Mexica*, which refers to the ancient Aztec people who established their empire in the Valley of Mexico in 1325 and ruled the entire region until the coming of Hernan Cortés in 1519.

In the novel, Alicia Ramirez, a caricature of my own mother, is the mother of the deceased Vietnam veteran, Jesse Ramirez. Jesse was her oldest son, the first of three children, and was deeply bonded to his mother, as his father's unfaithfulness was widely known in the *barrio* they lived in, El Cielito, a duplicate of my own, Sonorita Barrio. His father's relationship with his mistress had produced two children, and Jesse had confronted the woman's oldest son—a violent exchange that deeply disturbed his mother. It was then, that Jesse decided to quit college and make himself an open target for the draft. Alicia's guilt over her son's anger with his father, which in her mind, led him to his death in Vietnam, would become the darkest wound she carried. She regretted deeply not leaving her husband, and ending her family's despair and humiliation.

Jesse's plane took off for Vietnam from Sky Harbor Airport in Phoenix, in 1968, and it was then that Mother and son promised something that would one day become a reality. They both sensed they would never see each other again, and as Alicia held Jesse close, she told him that the war meant nothing to her—nothing at all. She wanted him back in her arms again. It was his voice she longed to hear once again. Jesse, in turn promised his grieving Mother that she would one day hear his voice again, and without realizing it, a "pact" was made between them.

Many years later Alicia, now a frail, elderly woman, experienced a night in which she "heard" the sound of her son's voice and other men whispering to one another, and connected this with the promise Jesse had made to her at the airport. She then made a *manda*, the word in Spanish means a "promise" to God to get to the Vietnam Memorial Wall to honor her son, no matter what she had to do to get there. A *manda* is a very serious vow taken up in the Latino world as a cry before God for healing, or for the end of a terrible episode in one's life. In fact, once a *manda* is made, to *not* accomplish it would be disastrous for the one who made the vow. It would bring great displeasure from the Almighty and be a deliberate failing before God, or so the belief goes.

In my own work, I often find myself vowing to write a book "no matter what I have to do," and this reminds me of the same energy of commitment made by Alicia Ramirez in the novel. I tell my creative writing students that when I am "clicking in a manuscript," that is writing at a steady pace, I am "like a dog with a bone!" My energy is focused and one-pointed, and nothing would be able to disturb me, except an extreme situation. In fact, the experience is one of "losing time," as the hours and minutes seem to have little significance. Easily, I could write for fourteen hours straight and consider it nothing at all. There are times I look up from my work and wonder why the house is so quiet—what happened to dinner? Then a quick look at the clock reveals it is 2:00 a.m. No wonder I'm starving! I am learning *not* to do this any more as this type of "abandon" takes its toll physically as well as emotionally and spiritually.

Let Their Spirits Dance relates the story of love reaching beyond the grave as family members, accompanied by Jesse's friends and many others who will join their journey, travel in a cavalcade of cars toward the Vietnam Memorial Wall, ending the family's long years of regret, guilt and bitterness endured after Jesse's death. In a highly strange connection from the past, the image of a "wall," so vivid in the novel, was the subject of a poem I wrote when I was seventeen years old. My poem, "The Wall," described a mysterious wall I had built around myself that protected me from insensitive people, and from the darkness in the world. I entered it in a contest, and later found out I had to buy the book, *Pegasus*, that had hundreds of poems, each paid for by other naïve writers. I felt ashamed at seeing my poem along with hundreds of others, as if none of it mattered at all, and now I wish I could find a copy of the book! Still, it is strange that the image of a wall surfaced in my life long before I had ever anticipated it would be the central theme of my first novel.

America's Longest War

Let Their Spirits Dance, is a spin-off from one of the stories that emerged in *Fragile Night*, entitled, "Cobra." This story told the tale of a Chicano Vietnam veteran, and his wife, living in the present time and struggling with Cobra's (the vet's nickname) harrowing experiences in the jungles of Vietnam. Cobra brought to my mind the agony of the Vietnam vet, a young soldier, facing the dark reality of an unpopular war challenged by thousands of American protestors back in the States. In fact, the Vietnam War, "America's longest war," was never officially declared a war by Congress, but was termed a "conflict."

Writing this short story, brought me face to face with the Vietnam War, and for the first time in many years, I began to shed tears for our soldiers who had died so far away from home. There was a lament in me, a cry I had hidden inside my soul. I had forgotten it was there. I was surprised that the lament searched me out, surfaced from me in tears, in a sense of deep grief, and in a desire to resolve something I could not initially recognize. The deepest part of my being was in distress. Images rose in my mind: coffins coming home by the hundreds, draped in American flags; friends from school who had been drafted; the *barrios*, our Latino neighborhoods emptied of young men who were not in college, and did not join the protestors; mothers who had lost a son, and had become ill with sorrow, some to the point of death, and the faces of young American troops running and hiding, shooting and being shot at on television newscasts of the war. This I had seen and forgotten.

I Never Mourned Vietnam

The process of mourning is an intricate one. It is a time to stand speechless and let the soul express grief in whichever way it chooses. Mourning may manifest in tears, shouts, sadness, rage, and a variety of other emotions. None of these expressions alone can manage the process of mourning, as it can be a lengthy one, and involve a level of existence known only to the individual soul.

Over the years I have worked as a grief and loss counselor and have helped people maneuver their way through the tasks of mourning, which in the end bring acceptance and peace, a strange dance between the on-going sense of missing a loved one, and the reality of coming to terms with the death. The meaning of life is searched out, life is reviewed, current goals are scrutinized, and beliefs are shaken to their roots. There can be moments of deep darkness in which the soul engages in no activity at all, frightening times in which the individual is alone, distant from others, even if standing in a crowded room.

My original goal was to write a documentary entitled: "I Never Mourned Vietnam." I was convinced that as individuals and as a nation, we had not mourned the Vietnam War, and the process was way over due as millions were still suffering. The idea of doing a documentary was, thankfully, blocked when I took the advise of John Gutierrez, a colleague who worked exclusively with Vietnam veterans. He had spent several years counseling soldiers who suffered with PTSD (Post Traumatic Stress Disorder), and were having problems coping with life as civilians. His suggestion caused me to literally pause as is evidenced by the silence on the tape recorder. I was recording our conversation at a coffee shop, discussing my plans to do a documentary, when he said, "Stella, you're a powerful storyteller. Don't do a documentary, we have too many of those around. Why don't you tell us a story of a Vietnam veteran's family living in the U.S. now—in postwar Vietnam?" There was a long pause on the recorder, then my voice: "Can I use that idea?" And we both laughed together, knowing the story would center on family, and the "unfinished business" of saying good-bye to a loved one who had died in combat. I knew this was the story I would tell, and the "vow" to complete it became as real to me, as Alicia Ramirez's *manda* to get to the Vietnam Memorial Wall, or die trying.

Faced with the bitter memories of the Vietnam War, and determined to complete my own mourning process, I sought out families of men, Chicano/Latino men, who had served in Vietnam. I focused on Chicanos who are second, third generation in the United States and were the men I knew in the *barrios*. Other cultures were not overlooked. I did hundreds of interviews for the book and included Puerto Ricans, Central Americans, South Americans, Cubans, Anglos, African-Americans, Native-Americans, Asians and South Vietnamese veterans, as well as their family members. It was a long war, the men who served represented a huge diversity of ethnic groups.

I resolved to dedicate the book to the first soldier whose family I interviewed who had died in Vietnam, without knowing that the family of Sgt. Tony Cruz, my first interview, had an astonishing piece of information to share with me. They related to me that Tony had told them several times before he left for Vietnam in 1969, that someday he would be famous, and they would read about him in a book. In fact, he said he would make history. The odds that I would find the exact family whose son and brother had made such a prophetic statement are impossible to calculate. The Cruz family's revelation, fueled my enthusiasm and led me to understand that I was dealing with forces I knew nothing about, and that I had somehow been mandated to write the book. Once again, a prophetic message, this time Tony's, became my guide into the invisible world created by the aftermath of war.

The Vietnam Memorial Wall

The plot of the story emerged in my mind, and linked itself with the names of Vietnam veterans on the Vietnam Memorial Wall. I became convinced that I was to tell a story that would cause Americans everywhere to take another look at the Vietnam War and at the 58,000 plus names on the Vietnam Memorial Wall, and in this way complete a mysterious part of the mourning process directly linked to the names on the Wall. As a budding novelist, I felt at a loss as to how to begin the story, and concentrated instead on doing research, conducting interviews and taking trips to settings that I felt would be part of the book.

My flight back to Phoenix from the Vietnam Memorial Wall in 1997 was the first time I had ever boarded an airplane. When I was a child, no one ventured far from home. There was no reason to leave home, nor money with which to travel, and if travel was done, it was done by car. The trip to D.C. was done by U-Haul with my son and another writer, John Ruiz, who filmed the trip. We followed the route that the family would take in the book. It amuses me when people have commented that they "felt they were there" in my descriptions of the many states we crossed, because in fact, they were standing with my protagonist, Teresa Ramirez, Jesse's sister, (through my eyes) taking in the sunrise over the red rocks of Colorado, gazing at the flat grasslands of Kansas, and finally staring incredulously at the busy streets of D.C. as the cavalcade of cars made an impressive entrance into the nation's capital by the group of weary, exuberant pilgrims, with

Alicia Ramirez finally singing again, finishing the song interrupted during choir practice at St. Anthony's Church so many years ago by the news of her son's death.

You Same, Same TV

Traveling to Saigon was an experience that led me to actually see where our young soldiers had shed their blood. In June, 1998, with money won from a creative writing fellowship granted by the Arizona Commission on the Arts for *Fragile Night*, I traveled to Vietnam with my twelve year-old son, John, and a small group of American nurses. One of the group, Tom Myers, had been a medic during the war, and had done three tours in Vietnam. His remembrance of battles, sites and the terrible conditions suffered by the "grunts," that is the soldiers in the trenches, were invaluable to my research. Everything the guys had told me about Vietnam proved to be true: the heat, humidity, constant rain, beautiful landscapes, and the friendliness and poverty of the people were just as they had described.

I had no idea that the Vietnamese watch the Mexican soap operas piped in from Mexico City, everyday in Vietnam with the dialogue translated into Vietnamese. When they saw my son and me walking into the lobby of the hotel after our twenty-three hour plane trip, they were stunned, and kept pointing to the T.V and the Mexican *novela* they were watching, and back to me. "You same, same T.V.!" they said, excitedly. I kept telling them, "I'm from the U.S.—America, Uncle Sam. I'm American!" But they insisted, "You same, same T.V., you Mexico!"

I figured they were partially correct, as some of my ancestors have come by way of Mexico, so I said, "Me, Mexico!" And they were elated. In fact, everywhere I went in Vietnam, they greeted me with, "You, Mexico!" Their pronunciation of the word *México*, was done with a correct Spanish accent, and this was attributed to the fact that their language was written by a French priest, and has as its base, Latin. Connecting with the people of Vietnam reminded me of what the Latino soldiers had told me during interviews, describing how difficult some of their missions were to the small villages. They related that the people who were supposedly enemies, looked like their parents and grandparents who had worked in the fields on farmlands in Mexico, and in rural communities across the U.S.

Mom's Passion Vine

Back in Phoenix after my trip to Saigon, I knew I had to begin the novel, and had absolutely no idea how this was to be done. I looked over the boxes of research and photographs, hundreds of pages of notes on my trip across the country and to Vietnam, interviews, books, tapes, sketches of the novel, and shook my head in despair, not knowing how to start a story that spanned thirty years of American history.

It was at some point shortly after my arrival from Vietnam, and after hours of frustrating starts and stops, that I sensed a desire to form something with my hands. I am not an artist who works with paint or clay, and I was confused. The urge was so great, that I finally took an ordinary piece of typing paper and began to crumble it this way and that. I set the wrinkled product on my desk in the utility room I used as an office at home, sat back and stared at it without one clue as to what it was, except that it looked like a flower. Finally, a thought from deep within surfaced to my conscious mind: *It's the passion flower your Mom had when you were a kid.* The memory of the passion vine my mother grew in our front yard when I was a child rose vividly in my mind. The image brought a revelation to my conscious mind that would prompt the next level of work on the novel.

The passion flower which clusters abundantly on a vine climbs gracefully on a trellis or wall, and depicts the passion of Christ. It is a huge white and purple bloom that has in its center what looks like a crown of thorns, nails, and tendrils that resemble whips. The petals symbolize the ten apostles at the crucifixion, and the five-lobed leaves, the cruel hands of the persecutors. Once I *recognized* the flower, or shall I say understood the revelation, I called my older sister, Rosie, who was a gardener like my mother. It was ten o'clock at night, but at that point, time had no meaning for me. All I wanted to know was if Rosie knew anything about the passion flower. "Wait a minute," she said, "let me go get my plant book." There was a pause on the other end. Then her voice came over the line. "I've got a book here, and there's a big blow-up of the passion flower all over the back cover." I said to her. "Hold that book, I'll be right there."

It was almost midnight when I picked up the book. I drove to my old *barrio* where my sister and her husband lived, and knocked on their door, frightening Rosie as she thought it was the cops! She looked at me, her eyes searching my face, "What's wrong?" she asked. "The book," I said, "the one with the passion flower—I need it." She rushed over to her kitchen table grabbed the book and gave it to me, her eyes telling me she thought I was crazy to come out so late at night to get the book. I drove home in a rush, and don't even remember stopping for red lights until I got home. Opening my computer to the first page of the novel, I wrote the beginning paragraph, describing the passion vine blooming until late November the year Jesse died. From the very first page, the passion flower connected readers to Jesse's death.

The first scene was of Jesse's sister, Teresa, my protagonist, standing, early in the morning, facing the passion vine that climbed to the rooftop of her parents' house, covering her mother's bedroom window with blooms, a duplicate of Mom's passion vine. By her side, was an old family dog, Duke, also reminiscent of a favorite family pet by the same name. Teresa was in deep mourning, weeping over her brother's death in Vietnam.

Filled with despair over the loss of her brother, Teresa had one thing in mind each morning: she would crush the beautiful blooms of the passion vine, as she did not want to be reminded of suffering, pain and death. She remembered Jesse's words, said to her before he boarded the plane for Vietnam, telling her that he didn't think he'd be coming back. He had vowed her to secrecy, and had asked her to take care of their mom. Her brother's words caused a great dilemma in

Teresa. How could she live with such a secret? And why had her brother entrusted her with the painful message? On this particular morning, Teresa chose *not* to crush the bloom she held in her hand, and silently let it go, opening herself to her own healing process.

Had someone told me, "Someday you will write a novel that will begin with a description of your mom's passion vine," I would have argued that it made no sense to me as Mom's passion vine had blown away in a thunderstorm when I was still a child. How could something I had not thought about in decades fill my mind so profoundly as to become the first words of anything I would ever write? But that is exactly what happened. Describing the passion vine in the first paragraph opened the whole novel to me, as if one of the wondrous blooms of the passion vine had just been placed in my hand. The passion flower had given me the key to the heart of the novel. It would be a novel of love, loss, suffering, unfinished business, the fading beauty of life, and finally transformation as each passion flower blooms for only one day. Each new day brings more blooms and a deep sense that life will survive even as death beckons.

I often tell my creative writing students to pay attention to things from "left field," things that don't make sense. These usually come in images that may seem ridiculous, or crazy, or they may come in words or sentences that seem disjointed and don't appear to fit into the current manuscript. The writer within does not follow our linear world, stories are circular, and thoughts may come in twists and turns that seem to have no logic. TAKE THE RISK! Had I not followed the urgent need to "do something with my hands," nor the trail leading me by coincidence to my sister's doorstep, I would have missed the possibility of connecting with the passion vine, which dramatically opened the novel in a way I could have never imagined.

Revelations arise in our minds from memory, dreams, thoughts, visions and current events to help us realize a truth. Something hidden within, reaches our conscious minds and we understand its message. A revelation, in many ways, is identical to an "aha experience," or a catharsis in which repressed, or hidden feelings and thoughts surface in the conscious mind in a new and profound manner.

There were times during the four years spent writing this novel, that I thought I might change the beginning, and start something new, and each time my inner being declared a definitive, resounding, *NO*. The beauty of the passion flower permeated the novel, here and there and gave it the intensity and intimacy I needed to describe the suffering and strange beauty that sprouts from pain. The family would transform in a wondrous, magical way as they traveled to the Vietnam Memorial Wall, facing their nightmares, their displaced hopes, the darkness of losing Jesse, and they would find redemption, and regain their beauty in a way similar to the passion vine sprouting new blooms each day.

"Entity Experience"

Once I began writing the novel, there was no turning back. By December 2000, I had submitted the manuscript to an agency in New York City who had asked to see the entire novel. I did not hear from my agent, Loretta Barrett, until months later. By March 2001, I became impatient and was ready to send out the novel to publishing houses, as I knew it would somehow get published, and was stopped in my tracks by a fellow teacher at Carl Hayden High School who insisted I seek an agent. "Get an agent!" he would demand over and over again. I'm grateful I took his advice to heart as he had graduated from Columbia University with an MFA (Masters in Fine Arts) and had actually read through my manuscript. "I'm small potatoes," I said to him, one day, and he replied, "Not for long!"

During that time, I had a trip planned with my children to Puerto Peñasco, also known as Rocky Point, which is a seaside city in Mexico that borders Arizona. In the wee hours of the morning, before our departure to Rocky Point, I was awakened from sleep, and did not sense the usual preoccupation with travel details, and arrangements for pets, etc. that go along with taking a trip. My son and grandson were asleep in the house, and all was quiet. I seemed to be drifting within, and in a state of perfect peace. I got up to get myself a cup of tea, as I had been suffering from allergies and wasn't feeling well. It was 2:00 a. m. in the morning. Outside it was rainy and unusually cold for March in Arizona. My thought was to cancel our trip, yet I knew I needed the time away.

As I sat on the edge of my bed drinking the cup of tea, I sensed an energy enter the room. I did not see anything with my physical eyes, yet, there was a definite energy that I could sense, filling the room, and I "followed it" with my eyes, as it seemed to form a semi-circle in my bedroom. An unseen group had entered my room. It was evident that this was not a single "entity," but several who now stood before me. Then, to my surprise, the following words formed themselves in my mind: *A decision has been made concerning you in other quarters.* The message was so clear that I repeated it out loud. "A decision has been made concerning me in other quarters." Later, I wrote the words in my journal and pondered over them, seeking an answer. But for now, I simply repeated the words, then lay down on my bed. It was as if the energy, or "entities," as I later called the energy, was telling me: *You can go to sleep now.* I remember rolling over on my side, and as I did the halogen lamp, which had been on at a dim setting, seemed to fade off. I slept until my daughter, Deborah, who now lived away from home, rang the doorbell to wake me up for our trip to Rocky Point.

Invisible Directive

Next day, at Rocky Point, I did not tell my children what I had experienced because I knew they would not understand. I didn't understand what had happened to me, much less could I expect them to understand. In fact, I told no one about my "entity experience" until much later. I figured the message meant that either a fellowship I had applied for at Stanford had come through, or that Loretta Barrett would represent my book, and it would be published. There were three things, however, that were made quite clear to me. First, whoever it was who gave me the message, had been given special permission to do so—signifying that the message was an important one. Secondly, "they" knew everything about me, who I was, and what I had been doing. And thirdly, it was a done deal.

One week after the message, while taking a short nap in my bedroom after work, the phone rang. I picked it up, and heard this greeting: "This is Loretta Barrett from New York City. I'm calling for Stella Pope Duarte." I identified myself to her, and she began to tell me how impressed she and her staff were with my manuscript. She went on to say: "I made the decision to represent you last week, but I've been out of the country and was unable to call you until now."

The time in which Loretta Barrett had made the decision to represent my work coincided exactly with my "entity experience." I later found out that Loretta Barrett had worked with young soldiers coming back from the Vietnam War, and that she was very dedicated to stories related to the war. She had told her office staff to look for three things in a manuscript: 1) a multicultural theme, 2) a woman writer, and 3) anything related to the Vietnam War. A young man on her staff from Holland, ran excitedly one day into her office waving my manuscript in his hand, telling her, "Loretta, I've got all three!"

Now that I had an "invisible directive," things began to happen fast. Within weeks, the manuscript was bid on by eight of the top publishing houses in New York City, and world rights for publication of the novel went to HarperCollins, and Diane Reverend of Cliff Street Books. Later, I went over the message I had been given, seeking clarity, and realized that the use of the word "quarters," was soldierly in nature. In fact, I would never have spoken that way to anyone; however, someone in the military might use that terminology. Whether it was the spirits of deceased Vietnam veterans visiting me that early morning in March remains a mystery, however, the importance of the work has remained intact over these many years. The novel has been hailed as a one-of-a-kind in telling the story of a family living in post-war Vietnam, whose journey to the Vietnam Memorial Wall unites all American families who seek to find meaning amidst the loss and pain inflicted by war. A fan from Australia related it was the most beautiful book he had ever read—why wasn't it a movie? I've asked myself the same question numerous times as the novel was applauded for its cinematic qualities even before it was published, and has twice been optioned for movie rights. I tell my students; the third time is the charm!

Messages from all over the world have confirmed the healing, hope and return of love, after years of darkness that the novel has brought to thousands of families and Vietnam veterans as well as soldiers from other wars. I have received messages from Vietnam veterans who had never visited the Vietnam Memorial Wall, but upon reading the book were encouraged to visit, and wrote back thanking me for the inspiration they needed to complete their own journey back to their buddies, to finally make peace with the memory of the young soldiers who had died on the bloody hills of Vietnam.

I do not purposely seek spiritual, other-worldly experiences, especially those that might border on receiving messages from the beyond. I may "see" messages in my mind, or in dreams and interpret them as revelations and visions, or connect the dots of the invisible world in my daily life, and am comfortable with these communications, however, I do not seek psychic gifts, such as seeing auras, or having visions in broad daylight, or becoming a medium able to hear spiritual messages from the beyond. The message I received in such a strange manner before the book's publication was related to me with so much power, and its confirmation came so quickly that there was nothing left to say, except that what I had been told was the truth. I still wonder if the men on the Vietnam Memorial Wall had anything to do with giving me this message—and if they did, more power to them!

More Powerful Than Pain

As I take a look at the astounding facts that surrounded this manuscript, and how it came to be created, I continue to sense that the initial reaction I had about the Vietnam War, the tears, the sense of deep mourning, began a path in me that led me to Vietnam, and to the completion of the process of mourning that I had put on hold for so many years. It is only when we take courage and examine the dark regions of the heart where bitter memories dwell that we can look forward to a time when we will be free to accept what has caused the pain, and move on.

Questions asked by Teresa Ramirez, as she contemplated war in all its gory details through her brother's letters, caused me to realize another important aspect of suffering. As the Ramirez family drew closer to the Vietnam Memorial

Wall, Teresa wondered why they were pursuing such a painful experience. The Wall would remind them of their loss; they would see Jesse's name etched on the Wall, and begin to relive the anger and bitterness of losing him, *and* having his body transported by the U.S. Army to the wrong address, while they waited, deeply troubled, wondering why his coffin had not arrived as scheduled.

Unfortunately, there were times when this actually happened to men who had served in Vietnam, including Tony Cruz, as the war was a long one, and transporting so many bodies meant mistakes were bound to happen. Teresa's question makes sense in this context, as she asked herself if her family was now more powerful than pain, since they were in pursuit of it, instead of the other way around. Perhaps, Alicia's *manda*, and Jesse's promise were breaking pain's power.

The revelation of the passion flower led me to embrace the theme of suffering and loss at levels that would pose questions and bring a deeper understanding of what it means to suffer. Loss brings about pain, internal pain that blends in easily with the invisible world within, and seems to disappear, yet is still very much alive, unless we have chosen to confront the memory and loss and allow healing to occur. Who suffers and to what degree remains another mystery.

In my mind, there is a huge reservoir of suffering in the universe, and every human being on earth will drink of it, from the tiniest baby to the oldest person on earth. Painful experiences that assault us with memories of loss, abandonment, betrayal, and a score of other human afflictions will remain for a lifetime, although at times the pain will seem to be forgotten, unless a person comes to terms with the pain and puts it in its correct perspective. The question Teresa posed about pain brings up an important aspect of facing painful memories.

If we do not run, and instead face the painful memory, pain lessens, and we begin to assume power over the experience. The antidote for a painful memory is this: *Yes, that's the way it was, but it's not that way anymore.* Now, I'm not in Vietnam anymore, or now, I'm not the six year-old being molested, or the young mom whose child died. Now, I have a chance to renew, and indeed to run ahead of the pain, deciphering it, courageously letting it "afflict" me again, but this time, as in the novel, the family is in control. Now they were ready and willing to face Jesse's death, and NOT run. This is powerful stuff, as I found out in interviewing veterans and their families from coast to coast, and in Vietnam as well. The "unfinished business," the Ramirez family had been living with for thirty years was being stirred up by *la manda's* magical power, but it was really, the courage of Alicia Ramirez that sent them racing to the Vietnam Memorial Wall to face their darkest time.

I have come to the conclusion that: *It's not what you suffer, but how you suffer it that makes you holy.* Life guarantees us suffering, but it gives us no road map on how to endure it. Each person chooses *how* they will suffer. Will it be in anger and bitterness, with hatred and revenge? Will the suffering turn the person into a devil, or a mad-man, or someone they never thought they would become? Often a child, raised in an abusive environment will grow to never know their own strengths, their own beauty, their own capacity to turn suffering into holiness, and that is another form of suffering: the loss of self. The truth is, we are all masters of pain and suffering. *We are wired to endure.*

In my mind, suffering involves an exchange, a giving up of something deadly, in order to come into a higher realm. I realized this, as I sat one day at lunch, at a small café on Central Avenue as I was writing *Let Their Spirits Dance.* The place was empty, except for myself sitting at one of the small tables. Suddenly, I felt a warm spot on the table, and touched it several times, noting its unusual warmth. I wondered if a hot plate, or a cup of coffee had rested there, but none of that was in evidence. I even peeked under the table to see if there was an electric plug connected somewhere under the table—there was none. Always conscious of things coming from "left field," I instantly took out a piece of paper from my purse and began to reflect thoughts that would be given to my protagonist, Teresa.

There was a debt owing in Teresa's life, as her family journeyed to the Vietnam Memorial Wall, but it had nothing to do with money. The universe cannot be conned by money! The debt was one of tears, pleas, a huge terrible energy she owed the universe that would cause an exchange to happen: a cold, bitter heart would be the payment for the strange warmth of forgiveness and love that was to follow. Interesting, how we hang onto the things that destroy us, and when we decide to give them up, we receive their opposite. Anger appears as a powerful emotion, yet it is dismantled by love. Without the exchange, there can be no transformation—a strange payment, indeed. Teresa's cold, bitter heart would find warmth again. My lucky day, to sit at a table with a mysterious warm spot that would connect me with invisible debts owed to the universe!

Time Travelers

How long can a ballerina dance? The question of being stuck in suffering is brought up in the novel by a porcelain ballerina who spins around in a glass container filled with purple sprinkles. It was part of the merchandise owned by a band of gypsies who had set up shop next to the Two Doors Gospel Church in the family's old *barrio.* As the years passed by, the ballerina was transferred to a cabinet Alicia Ramirez bought at a second-hand-store to display Jesse's medals. When turned upside down, the purple sprinkles floated over the ballerina making it seem as if she was guarding Jesse's medals. Teresa Ramirez, poignantly compared the memory of the passion flower to Jesse's medals; they both told the story of blood, death and murder. The unnamed ballerina, spun around in her glass container, silently guarding the medals unaware that they would not be there if blood had not been shed, and she would not be there either, as the cabinet had been bought to display the medals. Her spinning reminds us of the family's unfinished business with war and death. They had spun around in circles for years, avoiding the pain of Jesse's death, and now, dust had settled on the ballerina and the medals through the crevices between the cabinet's tiny doors. No matter how hard we try to avoid pain, like dust, it will find its way into our lives.

Revelation, upon revelation, like an enormous cluster of "blooms" in the form of related ideas, memories and themes reached my conscious mind, prompted by the image of the passion vine. The meaning of time itself was brought up in the novel in the chapter entitled, "Time Warp." Michael, the family's whiz kid, who at times brought his own brand of humor into the story, created a web page for his grandmother, and researched into parallel universes and Einstein's Theory of Relativity. His findings astonished his aunt, Teresa, with the fact that objects traveling at the speed of light experience time differently. In space there is no time, as we know on earth, and points of reference: vertical, horizontal, up and down, are obliterated by lack of gravity and the immensity of space. In the distant future, astronauts who travel into space for extended periods of time will find that time will not pass for them as their space ships travel at the speed of light; they will not age as they do on earth. If the voyage is a long one, perhaps they will come back younger than their own children or grandchildren!

On earth, each person experiences a different "passing of time." For those who live meaningful, and purposeful lives time may seem to pass too quickly, while those with little to do or think about, may experience life passing at a slower pace. It is true that when in the presence of someone you love, or someone who is very interesting, time seems to fly, and when in the presence of someone who brings discord, time passes too slowly. The Ramirez family was traveling in a time warp;

they were following an orb. They would travel through time, back to the past, and return to the present—changed.

We are time travelers, here on earth for a short span of time and destined for spiritual dimensions we know nothing about. At any point in time, we can realize a truth, taken out of context in our lives, as in the message of the passion flower, hidden within my internal world for decades, until the moment I needed it to unravel truths I would share with thousands throughout the world. Never underestimate a message that seems obscure or meaningless until you have explored its depth for greater truth and have humbly "stepped aside" to let its energy guide your work. Parallel universes co-exist with us, as is now being proclaimed by many current scientists, and Michael's admission that Uncle Jesse was "traveling" alongside them, was not far from the truth.

Bats and a Polished Eye

Another revelation, similar to that of the passion flower appeared in my conscious mind one day while I was busy writing a chapter of the novel, and from it came one of the most powerful, mystical characters of the entire work: Don Florencío.

I began suddenly to think of bats—the kind that fly at night, searching for blood. I could not shake the image of the bats, and being a bit more experienced in deciphering the language of the writer within, I closed the chapter I was working on, and opened a new document. I began to describe bats flying off in a frenzy, hungry, searching for blood, and began to write about them. I could see them in my mind, flying out of a cave. My mother had related to me that in the old days, people lived along the Rio Salado, also called the Salt River that ran through the south side of Phoenix. Some people were so poor, that at times they lived in nearby caves, or huts made of adobe and thatch. As I wrote about the bats and thought about what Mom had said, I began to create one of the most compelling characters of the novel; an old man living along the banks of the Salt River who chased bats that flew in a frenzy out of a cave. He was weeping, praying for the end of the war.

In vivid animation, almost like a movie, I could see Don Florencío, hands flapping in the air, chasing the bats out of La Cueva del Diablo (The Devil's Cave), weeping over the deaths of so many young men, huge losses for the families in the *barrios*. It was the night Jesse's plane had soared into the distant horizon, taking him to war, and the old man was directing the screeching bats to Vietnam, where blood ran freely. His tears were shed to attract God's attention, perhaps in this way He would stop the war, the old man reasoned.

Don Florencío stopped me in my tracks. For three months I researched the ancient seers of the Mexica (Aztec) nation, finally settling on one healer in particular who had special powers for seeing into the workings of the human heart. He was a healer of trapped souls and could accurately prophecy the future. He was called a *tlachisqui*, (letter 'l' is not pronounced) and that became the title of the 4th chapter in my novel.

I could have never imagined that one of my chapters

would be entitled: "Tlachisqui," I didn't even know what the word meant, until I completed the research. Then a host of related themes came to mind such as, the ancient world of Aztlán from which the Mexica nation had migrated somewhere north of present-day Mexico, possibly in the United States. From this "land of whiteness," they had journeyed following their war god, Huitzilopochtli, looking for the sign that indicated where they were to build their city. They would see an eagle perched on *el nopal,* (a cactus) with a serpent in its beak, or so the prophecy related. This sign finally appeared, and the people settled on marshland, in what would become the Valley of Mexico and built the imperial city of the Mexica nation, Tenochtitlan in 1325, which is now modern-day Mexico City.

The story went on to reveal that Quetzalcoatl, the peaceful god had been ousted from the tribe by the war god, Huitzilopochtli, but had vowed to return in a 1-Reed Year. According to Mexica calculations, the time of the Spanish conquistador Hernan Cortés's arrival on the shores of Cozumel was a 1-Reed Year, 1519. The prophecy proved to be correct, as the Emperor Moctezuma's empire fell at the hands of Quetzalcoatl, alias Cortés and his Indian allies.

Don Florencío was the one to tell Teresa and Jesse the history of their ancestors, and connect readers with the intriguing story of the conquest of Mexico and the beginning of a new race of people of European and Indian blood, *mestizos* (half white, half Indian), who would become the modern-day Mexicans and Chicanos. Don Florencío gave the novel another important symbol, that of the Ixpetz, or polished eye, which the old seer said Jesse Ramirez possessed. According to Don Florencío, he had seen an image of a warrior with a plumed headdress in the flames of his campfire just as Jesse's grand-father, Tata O'Brien (a duplicate of Tata Pope), had arrived to tell him Jesse had just been born. Don Florencío saw magic in Jesse's birth. He said Jesse had been born with the ancient "polished eye," the Ixpetz. With this gift, he would be able to see through the nature of things and understand their meaning.

In the novel, Don Florencío played a pivotal role as one who was able to tell Teresa that her brother would come back in a new form, as their ancient ancestors had always walked the earth. Traveling to the Vietnam Memorial Wall, Teresa remembered the old man's words, and one more thing—the tea he had offered her, *yoloxochitl*, the yellow flower of the heart to heal her broken heart, *tlazotlaliste*, (the fever of affection), and restore her ability to speak again, as the trauma of her brother's death had caused her to lose her own voice. I often think of what a world of history, culture and myth I would have missed by *not* following the bats! In fact, so powerful was Don Florencío that I had to literally "sit him down," and tell him he could not take over the entire manuscript. He finally settled for rising up here and there in the story, and at the end of course, he makes one more huge grand entrance.

The Dark Virgin

Don Florencío is not the only figure I attribute to the magical image of the passion flower blooming within, opening my mind to impossible new characters, images, ancient history, beliefs and customs. Like a huge constellation in my mind, more dots were to be connected leading me to one of the Latino world's most enigmatic and sacred figures: La Virgen de Guadalupe.

La Virgen de Guadalupe permeates my novel with her motherly charm and power. In fact, when this image rose in my mind, I felt it was a natural fit for the Ramirez family, as the Virgin of Guadalupe is the feminine, spiritual icon of the Latino world. She is called the "Dark Virgin" as her appearance in Mexico, ten years after the conquest by the Spaniards, revealed a young woman dressed like a Mexica princess, her skin as dark as the man who related seeing her, Juan Diego, a Mexica who had just converted to Christianity. He spoke Nahuatl, the ancient language, and so did she. In this way, she identified with the downtrodden Indians, victims of Spanish cruelty. Memories of my own attendance at La Virgen's feast days, and seeing the altar decorated with roses of every color, reminiscent of the flowers Juan Diego had gathered on the last day of the Lady's appearance, came vividly to mind. A magnificent basilica was built in her honor in Mexico City, and is visited by millions every year.

Faith in La Virgen's motherly protection led the Ramirez family on. Alicia and her friend, Irene, whose son had also been killed in Vietnam, clung to her for support as they journeyed to the Wall, and the Sodality of the Guadalupanas, an ancient sisterhood dedicated to the Dark Virgin, made a memorable appearance, led by Nana Esther, at the head of their procession. Teresa remembered the procession of mothers, walking slowly towards the altar, decorated with white linen and roses at St. Anthony's Church on December 12, La Virgen's feast day. With veiled heads, and rosaries dangling in their hands, the procession of mothers swayed as one, holding high the banner of La Virgen, trimmed in red, white and green, the colors of the Mexican flag. The presence of this group of women brought back sublime memories of my own, and prompted me to interview women who currently belong to the ancient sodality.

The Guadalupanas are known to wear golden medallions of La Virgen de Guadalupe, and satin ribbons, red, white, and green—that hang like tassels over their shoulders. They are buried with their medallions, and ribbons, and the custom is to have one Guadalupana standing at the head of the coffin, and one at the foot, as "guardians," until the body of the deceased member is buried. Such is their loyalty to La Virgen and to one another. Readers share in this special comradeship, and at the end of the novel, they witness the full release of the power of the sisterhood of the Dark Virgin.

Whatever comes to you from "left field," as you write, let it image in your mind. If you don't understand its meaning, be patient. Ask, ponder, reflect and soon the revelation given to you will become more concrete as it fills your conscious mind with layers of connecting memories, visions, history and characters that will tell your story as it has never been told before. I often wonder what in the world I would have written, had I not stopped to let the revelation of the passion flower lead the way for me. Under-estimating the power of obscure images is a mistake. They may lead you blindly at first, then as you allow your work to take form, the words like so many threads, will weave a delicate tapestry gathering your characters into a world, so real, so rare, it will take your breath away.

6

THE DARK, RED ROOM:
CONFIRMATION DREAM

"They take these girls somewhere, and they torture them."

Ramona Ortiz, Juárez News Reporter

How do writing ideas come to your mind? Is it from a haphazard conversation heard on a bus or subway, or in family talks at the dinner table? Is it something you see on television or hear over the radio? How many times do you turn within for writing projects? Are you comfortable seeking answers from your dreams, or from the invisible writer within as images are presented to you that may make no sense at all? These are questions I have learned to ask myself and other writers over the years.

My first introduction to the heinous crimes committed against women in the sister city of El Paso, Texas, Ciudad Juárez, Mexico came to me through news reports, the internet, and documentaries related to the "crime of the century," as the murders have been labeled by activists and concerned citizens throughout the world. In October 2003, as I presented from my work at St. Mary's College and Notre Dame University, I decided to go over information Notre Dame had in their files on the murders in Juárez, and found an article in the Observer, (2000) that described the murders of three young friends, ages, 16, 17, and 18, in a remote desert site outside of Ciudad Juárez. The girls had been buried in shallow graves, their arms and legs chopped off, and each body arranged in the shape of a cross. They had been raped, mutilated and killed. Their maquiladora (American factory) uniforms were discarded nearby. I was horrified. I could not believe that such a thing could happen to these young women who had absolutely no way of escaping their murderers.

What Attracts Your Attention?

I am attracted to helplessness. Whenever I find that someone is being cruelly treated: raped, beaten, tortured, or humiliated, it is all I can do to contain the strong emotions that rise within of wanting to instantly do something to help the victims. In fact, one of the workshops I do in conjunction with my research into the Juárez murders, is entitled: "We Cannot Look Away: Exploring a Social Conscience Through Writing." It is an in-depth look at the things that each of us simply "cannot look away from." What is it that disturbs you? What is it that *you* cannot look away from? Writers must uncover what is important in their work and seek ways to express their deepest understanding of right and wrong, evil and good through their own unique writing style. And this is a challenge.

After reading about the three young friends so brutally murdered, I made another vow—that I would tell their story, no matter what I had to do! I would honor: Esmeralda Juárez

Alarcon, 16, Juana Sandoval Reyna, 17, and Violeta Mabel Alvidrez, 18, through my work. Before my eyes, a multi-patterned tapestry began to unfold, revealing an intricate design that would help me understand the depth and breadth of what it would mean to write about the brutal femicides, (hatred against women) that were drawing international attention.

Not long after my return from Notre Dame, I visited the classroom of a dear friend, Dr. David Foster, professor of Women Studies at Arizona State University. One of the questions asked by a student was if I would write about the women of the middle east, as we are at war in that region, and I found myself answering: "Yes, perhaps someday I will, but right now, I am working on the story of the women of Ciudad Juárez." The students were very knowledgeable of the murders, and were glad to know I would be researching there, and writing a book about the women.

I have found that my writing process begins with my *thinking* about the subject I am interested in, mulling it around in my mind and coming to terms with the subject matter. Often, during walks, or while exercising, meditating, or early in the morning before I rise from bed, thoughts become crystal clear, and more links are made in my mind about the subject of interest, often accompanied by strong images. Then, I find myself telling someone about my idea, with caution at first, and maybe to only a few select people I trust. All of this is leading up to a verbal commitment, such as the one spoken in Dr. Foster's class as the work takes on its last final "aha." It is then that I am convinced it is something I will accomplish.

I walked away from Dr. Foster's classroom that day, rushing to get to my car before ASU security put a ticket on my over-due meter, telling myself out loud: "I'm going to tell the story of the women of Juárez!" Words, once said aloud, bring about another level of commitment. Now, it was time to prove my words true. Once again, the universe, God, angels, saints, dead writers, (and whoever else) went into action, or so it seemed to me, and things began to happen fast!

The Dark, Red Room

Dr. Foster told me he had an assistant that year, Ramona Ortiz, a woman completing her doctorate who had been a journalist for *El Diario*, a prominent newspaper in Ciudad Juárez. Would I be interested in interviewing her? Of course, I thought this would be an excellent idea, and quickly called the reporter and made an appointment to see her. The night before I was to meet her, I had a dream. It was December 6, 2003, and I dreamed of a dark, red room where atrocities were being committed. Someone was suffering there. It was a place of diabolical evil. I woke up troubled, wondering where in the world this place existed. Instinctively, I knew the dream was not referring to a place within me, which is the first metaphorical element I look at in interpreting dreams. Is the dream pointing to something within myself? In this case the dream was referring to an actual place.

The next day, December 7, 2003, I went to see Ramona Ortiz, and she related that she had been investigating the Juárez murders for over ten years. She told me she had found an intriguing, very important detail of the crimes that had hardly been discussed at all. If a girl's remains were found, perhaps in March, and forensics were used to investigate the time of her murder, it would invariably be found that she had not been murdered in March, but at a later time, perhaps two or three months or more after her abduction. "They take these girls somewhere, and they torture them," she said. "I know this to be true." As soon as she said the words, in my mind, I saw the dark, red room in my dream, and knew that it symbolized the place she was talking about.

Watch your dreams as you write. Often a dream that comes to you while writing can become part of your work, or lead you in a new direction. *If I Die in Juárez*, relates the story of three young protagonists, Evita Reynosa, 13, Mayela Sabina 11, and Petra de la Rosa, 18 who, together, uncover a notorious cartel murderer. It is Petra who is the maquiladora (factory employee). She is abducted in the novel by a powerful cartel headed by Agustín Miramontes Guzmán, and finds herself in the dark, red room I saw in my dream. The reporter's words confirmed my own suspicion that the room I saw in my dream the night before the interview was an actual place. The atrocities then became real to me, and the dream of the dark, red room took a prominent place in the novel.

Hidden in the abductor's home, the dark, red room was used to torture young women and to make videos to be played later of their suffering. Here, my protagonist, Petra found herself utterly helpless. She often escaped through *dissociation*, a coping mechanism used by victims of abuse to protect their internal person from harm. At times, she saw herself flying above the bed, hiding in the globes of the chandelier, or resting in a dark corner of the room when the pain became impossible to bear. To Petra, her abductor was the legendary monster, *el tsahuatsan*, a seven-headed serpent that would roam the mountains close to her childhood home. The *tsahuatsan*, was chased by thunderbolts, and would fall to earth, forming lakes that would trap its victims and drown them. In her mind, Augustín Miramontes Guzmán was *el tsahuatsan*, but what he created in the dark, red room, were lakes filled with her own blood.

As hard as it was to write the scenes of Petra in the dark, red room, how much harder was this horrific experience for the many young women who have suffered such a fate? Suffering, once faced, can come to an end, and this is always my hope in describing painful moments. In fact, each of my protagonists will rise, and become empowered in the story, realizing a new day, and fully embracing the possibility that one day the murders will end. Love will survive, and the reader will experience the true love between Petra and Luis Ledezma, as well as the abiding love of her parents, and grandmother, Teodora, who teaches her granddaughter a magical chant to the morning sun, an act of gratitude for the gift of life so generously bestowed by God upon their ancestors, the Tarahumara Indians.

I pledged to myself that my readers would, "walk in the shoes of my girls," and hundreds of messages sent to me by readers from all over the U.S. and from other countries as well, prove that they have truly walked the raw and haunting streets of Ciudad Juárez, and have also experienced the courage my girls felt as they united to face an ordeal that would challenge the bravest among us.

Finding My Way to Juárez

As I began writing, *If I Die in Juárez*, I was working as Chair of Counseling for a counseling department that served over 2,500 teens at Cesar Chavez High School. Besides this, I was teaching at the University of Phoenix, and doing counseling at a local behavioral health center. I had little time to do anything during the day but administer services through my staff of counselors, office personnel, and community liaisons. One day I received a call from Francisca Montoya, a strong woman activist in the community who served as head of a resource center for women in South Phoenix. She asked if I would like to visit the center and see how we could coordinate services for the young women on our school campus. I agreed, and as we were sitting in her office talking, suddenly, I found myself blurting out.

"Francisca, I have to get to Ciudad Juárez! I'm writing a book about the women and the murders going on there."

Francisca looked at me, puzzled. "I'll go with you," she said, calmly.

"Don't say that, unless you mean it," I said. "I need to go now!"

"Oh, I mean it. I've worked there through a health program, and know people from Juárez. I know a family who can help you."

Within two weeks, in a rented car, I found myself driving with Francisca Montoya to Ciudad Juárez, the first of many times I would visit the city over a period of three years. I recall being ill with a cold, trying to make myself feel better with cough drops and hot coffee; yet not allowing any physical ailment to keep me from my trip. We traveled by night with Francisca driving. She had been to Juárez several times, and knew the road quite well. We were to leave our car in El Paso with a friend of hers, and be picked up by Piedad and her husband, Javier, both born and raised in Juárez. Piedad worked with an international health program that offered services on both sides of the border. She had once been an anchor woman for a television station in Mexico City, and her contacts throughout the city became crucial to my investigation. The couple, along with their three children, became my family in Ciudad Juárez, and without them I would not have been able to complete the research I needed to do.

Back in Phoenix, I was shown a list of the murdered women by another woman activist who had collected statistics and related information. Sheer horror rose in me as I read page after page, single-spaced, of hundreds of names of women who had been murdered. The number currently exceeds 500, with a great percentage of the bodies suffering mutilation. I simply could not believe it! On the list of women's names, one name caught my attention, it was the name: *Petra*. Inexplicably, I was drawn to the name, as it had surfaced in my mind over and over again, even before I had started writing the novel.

Again, when something comes to you from 'left field' and you cannot make sense of it, follow its trail. I knew no one named Petra, yet when I saw the name listed as one of the women killed in Ciudad Juárez, I pointed to the name and said out loud: "Here's my baby. She's gonna tell me her story." And thus was born the major protagonist of the novel, Petra de la Rosa. I did not "hear a voice," nor did I act as a medium to the world beyond, it was simply a "center" I had uncovered for the novel. My vow to write the book had been heard; I was being "helped" in ways I could have never imagined.

A Miraculous Beginning

The U.S. and many other nations have had a hand in causing havoc in Ciudad Juárez by setting up factories in border towns that draw laborers from rural communities, most of them women, who are likened to slave labor, as wages paid to them are so low, they cannot sustain a decent lifestyle. In addition to this, the huge smelter, ASARCO (American Smelting and Refining Company) that stands on the very edge of the border between the two cities is owned by the U.S. and has over the years contaminated Juárez with chemicals that have become a part of the land and water. The smelter, not in current use, was positioned in such a way, as to catch currents of wind and point them in the direction of Juarez, carrying black smoke and numerous deadly chemicals from the smelter's chimneys.

Three strong images came to my mind as I began the novel; first that of a young girl, Evita, who wanted nothing more than to live in peace; secondly, the image of a butterfly that Evita longed to become, and thirdly the image of Evita's little brother, Fidel, whom she adored, born an albino. The opening paragraph of the novel described one of Evita's dreams in which she experienced a huge gust of wind rushing in through an open door that took her by surprise. This was *peace*, although in disguise, and in her mind, it was a miracle, compared to her real life. Peace touched her and she suddenly felt as if she was protected by God, and nothing bad could happen to her. Her dream was in direct opposition to her real life on the streets of Juárez, as she lived daily in poverty, uncertainty, and fear. It was the first time Evita had experienced such a surge of power, and long after the dream had faded away, she kept a secret space hidden in her memory, guarding it for the hope that peace would return.

How the opening of the novel materialized in my mind remains a miracle. I had been struggling with how to effectively open the story with a passage that would somehow define the madness, and hope that was Juárez. I had all but given up one night, frustrated with many false starts, when I blessed myself with the sign of the cross, looked at a photo on the top shelf of my desk of my dear sister, Rosie, who had been my greatest writing ally in the family, and uttered a silent prayer. "Sis, help me, I need to start this novel!" I then closed my eyes and turned silently within, and the words of the opening paragraph flowed effortlessly. Turning, metaphorically, to my sister for help is one of several ways I have used over the years to center my own creative energy

Your own method for centering yourself in your work is of your own choosing. Perhaps, music unlocks the right side of your brain—the one that is infused with powerful images and insights, and that's how you get your own creative energy to the linear part of your brain—the left side, and thus produce writing. You may be the type who likes to sit outside on your patio and watch a sunset or listen to birds chirping away in the trees. You may release your creative energy through meditating, silent prayer, reading inspirational work, or through a variety of ways that engage your own creative spirit, and release words that are waiting for you to summon them into your writing. Creative writing is truly a miraculous process! I would advise you not to turn to a fellow writer, family member, or friend when your own creative energy is being summoned. GIVE YOURSELF A CHANCE. Later, you can edit, work on the rhythm and sound of the words, or have someone give you feedback, however, the initial contact with your creative energy should be your own. Your *own* creative energy, not someone else's, should lead your work. Internally, you are sacred ground, and the process by which you unlock your creative energy will be realized as you practice being true to your own "writer within." By being faithful to learning the language of your own soul, you will come to understand the metaphorical revelations, visions and dreams that rise within you, and will be able to sort them out and use them to make meaning in your work.

Images, Voice and an Albino

The image of a butterfly provided a beautiful and powerful symbol of freedom and escape in the novel. It came quickly, in the first chapter, as Evita, still in grammar school, drew a butterfly one day and imagined herself, full wings extended, flying safely overhead, away from the harsh world she lived in. Evita took two pieces of paper instead of one, as her teacher had directed, and drew a butterfly with huge wings. As she proudly presented the teacher with her drawing, she was humiliated and told she had wasted precious paper, and she was never to draw a butterfly that big again!

From that moment on, Evita never drew another butterfly, although the image remained alive in her soul. It would be Mayela, the youngest protagonist, the artist of the three, who would free Evita with her own painting of a butterfly so splendid, it would awaken in Evita the desire to be free again.

The child, Evita, longed to do one thing: escape the ugliness she saw around her. Yet she was held fast by poverty, society's judgments and the blundering mistakes of her mother. To add to the confusion of her life, came a figure so intriguing, he almost took over the novel, similar to the power Don Florencío had in *Let Their Spirits Dance*. Creating an albino was my way of shedding light on the deformities present in Ciudad Juárez, due to the contaminated landscape. Genetic features normal in the development of a healthy fetus are often compromised in Juárez due to poor health care and environmental pollution.

The baby albino, Fidel, born to Evita's mother, Brisa, was

so intriguing a figure for me that for a while the whole novel was centered around his existence. I followed the "albino track" for some time, frustrated at every turn. Then, once I saw I could not tell the novel through his eyes, I began to contemplate a novel told in first person by one of the protagonists. Again, frustrated by not having the liberty I needed to enter the minds of my other characters, including the cartel members, I turned to relating the story in third person, with each protagonist taking a part in the novel, and all of them uniting in Ciudad Juárez.

Each writer must make a decision as to which "voice" will be used in a piece of writing. The voice is not only the style of the work, it is also the author's distinct manner of telling the story. One technique that has helped me in creating immediate, fresh writing is to initially write the story in first person, even though, eventually it may turn into third person. First person captures the intimacy of each character in relation to self, others and the story in general. Personally, I am a workaholic, and it is nothing for me to write up to twenty versions of a work, and that is not including all the edits and rewrites!

Evita's baby brother was born with no pigment in his skin, and was a curiosity for reporters who visited at Evita's home hoping to catch a glimpse of the rare phenomenon. Evita was convinced she was from a family of freaks: her baby brother was an albino; her older brother had been badly burned in an accident; her sister, Lety had a bad hip that made her limp, and Evita was often described as the dot at the end of a sentence. In spite of Baby Fidel's deformity, Evita loved him dearly, and watched with fascination as his eyes seemed to change from blue, to green to yellow. She was crushed when Fidel drowned at the age of two, by falling into a bucket of water. It was then she decided that nothing beautiful could last for very long— like the butterfly she had drawn in school, her little brother, strange and beautiful, had been taken away from her.

Another major symbol to surface, boldly, in the novel was the sense of *el mestizo* rising; the Indian coming face to face with the proud, arrogant "conquistador" and winning out through a battle of sheer will. My own interest with the conquest of Mexico and the domination of the tribes by the fair-skinned Europeans, led by Hernan Cortés, prompted the creation of the cartel leader, Agustín Miramontes Guzmán, as the epitome of the harsh victimizer.

The reader is a witness to the creative process of rising again and again as experienced by the villagers of Montene-gro, the birthplace of Petra de la Rosa. The people of Monte-negro dug wells and captured rain water in iron tubs, and in this way resisted the rich and powerful European landowners who redirected the Rio Gris to their own farmlands. The rich had set themselves up as gods but they were only men, and now the *mestizos*, a mixture of Indian and European blood rose again and again, and in this way vanquished the ancient conquistador. At the end of the novel, again *el mestizo*, beaten down and bloodied, rises as Petra de la Rosa assumes her own eternal position in the universal cosmos.

Titles and Endings

One word about titles of books and endings; they often do not remain the same, and may in fact change before your very eyes—so *do not commit* to a title or ending to the point that you are no longer open to something new. My novels, so far, have not ended the way I chose, but the way the story wanted to end. A story has a "mind of its own," and is so powerful it will resist your efforts to make it do what *you* want it to do. The titles of each of my novels changed once the work was completed. A new title was given, and in spite of my own misgivings, the new titles were best. One of the most challenging things I have done as a writer is to stay out of the way of the story! Yes, humbly, let the story do as it wills, and you will be surprised at the route it may take.

Let Their Spirits Dance, was not the original title of my first novel; it was originally entitled: *Voices From the Wall*, however, my editor and agent felt the title was too common, the word "voices" was used extensively in many books, so right before publication, I received a phone call from my agent, and a new title was requested. I had only one weekend to come up with a new title, and I was frantic. I even went back to my old *barrio*, hoping to get some inspiration for the new title. I actually got off my car, dressed in business attire as I had been teaching a university class, and walked down the streets of my childhood neighborhood. I found out quickly that I no longer belonged there. Gone were the neighbors I knew as a kid, and the friendly environment I remembered.

I bought a Pepsi at one of two local Asian markets, and

asked the cashier if he knew the Yees, a Chinese family who had originally owned the store. I thought, perhaps he was one of their descendants. "I'm Korean," he said, irritated, "I'm not Chinese." I was greeted everywhere by the depressed surroundings, and by African-Americans and Latinos who looked at me suspiciously as I walked by. One young, black woman challenged me, thinking perhaps I posed a threat. A man was following me, hoping to get my attention, possibly to "pick me up."

After my walk through the neighborhood, I felt even more frustrated, and as I sat in my car, a thought came clearly to my mind: *The story is not about this place, it's about the human heart.* The revelation was correct. My novel spanned universal themes that encompassed peoples of every color and of every nation. Still, I had not come up with a new title.

Later that day, one name materialized over and over again in my mind: John Gutierrez, the same gentleman who had suggested I write a story and not a documentary. I could not get him out of my mind; so on Sunday night, I desperately called him up. I had not spoken to him in months and didn't even know if he was in town. Luckily, he answered the phone, and in a desperate plea I told him my situation. I needed a title by tomorrow, which was Monday, the book was going to the printing press in New York City. "Stella, just calm down," he said. "We'll figure this out." For some unknown reason I began to read to him from the last page of my manuscript. In the passage, Teresa was describing the culmination of the family's journey and was reflecting on the fact that in honoring their warriors on the Vietnam Memorial Wall, they had also exchanged orbits with them, and had let their spirits dance. After reading the passage, John said.

"There's your title."

"Where?" I asked, still not understanding.

"Let their spirits dance," don't you hear it? Listen—let their spirits dance."

I repeated the words over and over again, and each time I said the words, I knew John was right—that was the rightful title of the book! Next morning, I called Loretta Barrett in New York City, and my editor, now Rene Alegría, at HarperCollins, and told them, "I've got the title for my novel: LET THEIR SPIRITS DANCE, and they were as overjoyed as I was.

The title and ending for *If I Die in Juárez* took a mysterious turn as well. Originally, my ending had been different, but due to feedback from reviewers, who suggested a new ending. I reluctantly went back to the drawing board, and wrote a new ending, which was superior to the old one. The title of the novel, originally: *Sing to the Morning*, also underwent a major change, and came about through the words of Estevan de la Rosa, Petra's father upon his forced arrival in Ciudad Juárez.

Due to illness, Estevan, had been forced by his wife, Flor, and other family members to seek medical help in Juárez. He knew the evil of the city, and wanted nothing to do with it, and as he lay wearily down in a bed in the home of their cousin in Juárez, Estevan grabbed his wife's hand and pleaded with her to bury him in Montenegro if he died in Juárez. He repeated his request, holding tight to Flor's hand, unwilling to let her go, in spite of her tears, until she promised that if he died in

Juárez, she would bury him in Montenegro. His wife looked deeply into his eyes, knowing this was her husband's death wish, and she solemnly promised to do as he wished. Then, for the first time in the novel, Estevan smiled, comforted with the thought that one day he would rest peacefully in his own small village.

The title, *If I Die in Juárez*, is a prepositional phrase. A reader will "stumble" into the meaning of the title towards the middle of the novel, through Estevan de la Rosa's words, and in this way, the significance of "coming home" something precious to all humanity, breathes its own strength into the story, and reaches out to the reader with the universal theme of love beyond the grave.

Trust yourself, as the creator of your own work to know when the title and ending are right. If circumstances point to a different title or ending, *do not fear* to test the waters, you may find that a new title is "right under your nose," or that a new ending will capture the meaning of your work as never before.

❧

The image of the dark, red room set me on the right course in writing, *If I Die in Juárez*, even though I did not know how or where it would lead. Once again, the risk taken was worth all the doubts, anxieties and fears I had to overcome to write a novel that challenged me at every turn, and gave thousands of readers a once-in-a-lifetime look into a dark tale that would eventually lead through a series of harrowing twists and turns, back to the light.

7

ROSALIE MORENO: HEALING DREAM

You don't need a replacement for your sister,
she's still there. It's you who has to get
used to the new relationship.

HOW does death fit into the picture of who you are as a writer? This may seem a difficult question to answer, however, life and death are intricately woven into the pattern of our lives. We all experience very difficult times as we write, and one of the hardest for me, personally, was the death of my sister, Rosalie "Rosie" Moreno. Rosie was twelve years older than me, and became in many ways my second Mom. As a child, I remember watching her comb her hair and put on make-up and fancy clothes, transforming herself into a princess. By far, Rosie was the most beautiful of all my sisters, and I was mesmerized by her elegance and charm.

Over the years, Rosie's house became my "family home," especially after the death of my parents. Hardly a day went by that I did not talk to her, no matter where I was. My calls reached her as I traveled to Indiana, New York, Washington D.C., Maryland, Florida, Minnesota, Texas, Oregon, Colorado, New Mexico, on and on. She and her husband, Manuel, did not do much traveling, and lived a humble life, moving back to our old *barrio* after a series of financial losses cost them their family home. Rosie was an anchor for me; I knew she would be there when I dialed her number. I knew I could see her by simply visiting at her home. There, I would taste the delicious food she made, spend time dipping cookies into hot coffee, and sitting around talking, surrounded by her love, and the comradeship we shared as sisters and as soul friends. She was there for me as I began my writing life, and every step of the way, she was conscious of my work, and of what I was writing. Her positive response to my work was something I very much valued. She became what the ancient druids called an *anmchara*, (an-m-ha-ra) a Celtic word meaning a "soul friend," someone cultivated over a lifetime. The druids, who existed in ancient Ireland, and practiced their "pagan" religion even before Christianity had taken root on the Emerald Island, coined the phrase: *Anyone without a soul friend (anmchara) is like a body without a head.*

Indeed, this statement is true to this day. Without someone you can trust, someone who understands your heart and soul, you may sense yourself alone and disconnected from others, drifting and lonely. It is deep, intimate relationships that enrich our lives. My relationship with my sister gave my life purpose, and meaning. I felt loved and needed, and her opinions mattered more to me than the opinions of anyone else I knew. Often, we discussed our internal growth, referring to a book we had both come to love: *Letters of the Scattered Brotherhood* (Harper & Row, 1948), edited by Mary Strong, a collection of letters from all over the world on how to live rich, spiritual lives in one's daily existence. "I read today in the *Letters...*" would be a very natural way for us to begin a conversation. Neither one of us was afraid of telling it all to the other. We often talked about our mistakes, the darkest things we were thinking about, or had done, with no thought that the other would do harm with such private information. There was total trust. The mutual question between us was: "How's your soul today?"

Facing the Loss of My Anmchara

When Rosie died on August 13, 2002, I was devastated. She had told me she would wait for *Let Their Spirits Dance*, to be published, and she did. She was present at the celebration of the book's release, in May 2002, with over 400 people in attendance at Phoenix College. She loved the way the book was written and marveled at my writing talent, often buying me a ceramic angel who was busy reading a book, or writing on a scroll, to "take care of me." Where she found these ceramic angels is beyond me, but she would search them out, and give them to me. I have them in my office at home, and am now looking at one of them; a lovely angel, holding in her hands a tiny, white dove.

My first public event as an author, took place on November 3, 1997 after the release of *Fragile Night.* It was my birthday as well, and I was to share the stage at Bulpitt Auditorium on the Phoenix College campus with three other writers. I was a nervous wreck! I had taught adults in college and university classes, and had by then, been an educator in a variety of elementary and high school settings as well, however, I had *never* presented from a published book—this night would be my first.

I recall pacing back and forth, behind the thick stage curtain, as I went over my notes, which included giving thanks to my family, friends, and publisher for help in completing my first book. With hands ice cold, knees shaking, and my mouth as dry as a cotton ball, I walked out on stage. I made the mistake of reading, or attempting to read an entire short story, big mistake! There was no time for that, and I had to be reminded to get off the stage.

Rosie had coerced the family into attending, as I wanted to publicly recognize them from the podium. Most of my family members were not used to attending literary events, and wanted nothing to do with it. Rosie threatened, cajoled, and ended by promising them a party, which was something everyone in the family looked forward to at her home, so they came. Rosie was the one family member who took time to celebrate my successes, including my graduation from Arizona State University, insisting I walk in the university's graduation ceremony in full regalia, even when I myself did not want to. I finally consented to walking through the College of Education's ceremony, and afterwards, she had a huge party at her home to celebrate the first person in the entire family who had ever graduated from the university. She was so proud of all my accomplishments.

I don't think I could have ever understood what my sister's death would mean to me. My work over the years had included grief and loss counseling, and I thought I understood what it meant to experience loss and go through the steps of mourning, finally discovering healing and acceptance. To this day, I don't think I have ever wept as much for anyone as I did for Rosie. The day after her death, I simply could not get out of bed. My body was weary beyond belief, and each time I tried to get up, I would fall back on my bed.

My children were worried, as they had never seen me in this condition. Their so-called, "super mom," was now reduced to sadness and tears. My youngest daughter, Deborah, came by and did the simplest, most healing of things. She did not try to get me up, and instead, lay on the bed by my side, and held me close. Nothing was said between us, but I understood that she was there for me, in the tradition of the ancient Spanish words said to console the grieving: *Te acompaño en tu sentimiento.* (I accompany you in your pain.) Without realizing it, Deborah was offering me healing just by *being there.*

The Big Surprise

Each death we encounter comes with a distinct theme, or recurring thought about the person we have lost. In losing Rosie, I felt as if a part of me was missing; I could never replace her. This became the theme of her death, the sense that no one could ever take her place. At the hospice center the night of her death, Rosie told me how worried she was about her husband. What would happen to him? Would he be okay? I encouraged her, telling her that their children would help him, and he would be fine.

Then she said to me, looking directly into my eyes, "How would you like a big surprise tonight?"

"What kind of a surprise?" I asked.

She smiled gently, almost as if it was a joke between us. "If you go home right now, they're gonna call you up, and tell you I just died."

"Is that the surprise you want?" I asked.

"Yes," she said, once again showing a radiant smile on her weary face, "That's the surprise I want."

It was important for her to help me understand that she knew her death was upon her, and she had accepted it. "If that's the surprise you want, then that's the surprise I want too," I said, holding onto her hand. It would be the last time we would ever hold hands.

Previous to this conversation, my sister had related dreams she was having, many of them reflecting the end of her life. She would recount the dreams in detail, but never asked me to help her decipher their meaning. So sacred is each person's internal world, that I will not venture into it, unless I sense a person *allowing* me in. Interpretation of a dream belongs to the dreamer; we both understood what her dreams meant without needing to discuss them.

Rosie also recounted "seeing" Mom and our oldest sister, Linda, who had died a few years earlier. When I asked her where she saw them, she would simply say: "In the kitchen," or "in the hallway." When I asked her *how* she saw them, she answered, "As clearly as I'm seeing you." This was said with no alarm, or fear, and in a matter-of-fact tone as if we were discussing what was showing on T.V. All I could surmise, was that my deceased Mom and sister, Linda, were drawing spiritually close to her, offering comfort and guidance for her transition to the other world.

You Don't Need a Replacement

By the end of 2002, I was still struggling with Rosie's death, and had almost given up trying to deal with the grief. I was considering getting counseling, perhaps even medication as I felt I was exhibiting signs of a clinical depression. My zest for life was on hold, and in spite of national publicity and media attention across the nation and around the globe for *Let Their Spirits Dance*, I simply could not separate myself from the dark sense of loss.

On December 1, 2002, I had a dream. I dreamed I was at the fitness center working out, and saw Rosie standing close-by. She looked okay, a bit tired, but seemed to be fine. We were talking to one another. After my work-out, I walked out of the gym, and found that my car was missing. Apparently, it had been stolen. I walked back into the gym, asking if anyone had taken my car by mistake, and no one knew anything about it. I said aloud in the dream: "I'm gonna have to call my insurance company, and they'll have to get me a replacement, or give me the money for the car." I awoke from the dream, thinking I had to call my insurance company. Then, as easily as a ray of light penetrates the darkness, a revelation materialized in my mind, and I was granted the interpretation of the dream: *You don't need a replacement for your sister. She's still there. It's you who has to get used to the new relationship.*

The dream captured the pain I was experiencing, which was the sense that I could never "replace" my sister. I recall at her funeral a couple of people, seeking to comfort me said: "You have other sisters, don't you, Stella?" I could have shouted at them, "NOT LIKE THIS ONE!" They were correct, and my remaining sisters are a comfort, but each person is irreplaceable and truly no one else will ever take the place of a loved one.

The dream was challenging me, demanding me to take a closer look at what had happened. If I believed in God's power to restore our spiritual lives in eternal dimensions, then where was my faith? She was still there; it was me who had to come to terms with the *new relationship.* After realizing this wondrous message, I felt as if a ton of bricks had been taken off my shoulders, and slowly the spark of life from within was rekindled.

You're Next!

In 1994, after Mom's death, I recorded in my journal, a most significant healing dream that rescued me from the deep wound of losing a parent. As mentioned earlier in this book, my mother made a decision to come to my house to die. She had asked me specifically to bring her to my home, and it was an honor to do so. Dedicated to La Virgen, Mom predicted she would die on one of the Blessed Mother's feast days, and she was correct. Her death came on August 15, 1994, a special day honoring the Blessed Mother.

After Mom's death, I became physically ill. Every joint and bone in my body ached with pain so severe I could barely walk, or even turn the ignition key in my car! My whole body was inflamed and my hands and feet swollen. I was shocked at the pain that had taken over my body. My mother had died in great pain; one of her ailments, osteoporosis, had caused her intense pain throughout her body and towards the end, she had lost the ability to sit up, stand or walk. In fact, my mother's body was bent almost in half from the deformity caused by osteoporosis in her spine. Now, I her daughter, was exhibiting her pain. It was my body's way of mourning my mother—totally identifying with her suffering. Finally, I found relief through my doctor's use of steroids, a short-term treatment that brought the terrible symptoms under control. But it wasn't over. The theme of my mother's death was a sentence I could not get out of my mind: "I don't know how to live without my mother."

These words plagued me, causing me great distress. Here was a Mom I had loved so deeply since I was a child, and now she was gone. I had never known a day without her, and now had no idea how to live the rest of my life without her presence. A powerful healing dream came to bring peace out of chaos. One night, a few months after Mom's death, I dreamed that I was in what looked like a house, and I was talking to Mando, an old friend of mine from childhood. I was telling him, "You know Mando, I don't know how to live without my mother." As I said the words, entering into the room, I saw my mother with Linda, (not deceased at the time) at her side. I recall seeing Mom's wispy white hair, and her simple house-dress. Then I heard a booming voice: "YOU'RE NEXT!" I said aloud, "I can't be next, I'm one of the babies of the family!"

I awoke from the dream with those terrifying words sounding in my mind: "YOU'RE NEXT!" I again repeated what I had said in my dream, "I'm one of the babies, I can't be next!" I was taking the dream literally, and of course, that is a mistake. Dreams speak to us in metaphorical language, I had forgotten for the moment. Then, instantly, rising into my conscious mind, came the revelation. I had been asking how I was to live without my mother, and the dream was "shouting" at me: *That's how you live without your mother, as if you're next. Everyday of your life, live to the fullest, giving and receiving love. Live as if any day on earth could be your last—that's how you live without your mother—as if you're next!*

❧

My healing dreams centered me on love's ancient mystery: we live *because* we are loved, and we live to love others. Such is the power of the healing dream, and its power, may not be fully understood in this world. We may have to wait, until we can see one another face-to-face in spiritual dimensions to uncover the entire truth. Keep alert for healing dreams as they possess the power to cause you not only to regain what was lost, but to restore your soul and change you into someone new.

8

WRITING TWO BOOKS AT ONCE: NEW BABY DREAM

Someday, we will all be invisible.

ELECTRICITY could never travel as fast and as efficiently as messages from the invisible world. We each carry the possibility of understanding millions upon millions of thoughts throughout our lives, and these "understandings" can come in flashes of seconds that cannot be calculated by the most sophisticated instruments. But how does this happen? There are millions of people throughout the world who live their lives, and never seem to understand their purpose on earth, never seem to respect their internal person, nor do they have a craving to explore their own internal landscape. Judgment is not an option, nor should it be a part of how we relate to others. No one knows why one person chooses to respond, or has the capacity to respond, and another does not.

C.S. Lewis has stated it very poignantly in his words: "The greatest difference between any two people is that one has decided to grow, and the other has not." Our desire to grow spiritually has nothing to do with economic status, ethnicity or ambition. There are reasons both visible and invisible, some reaching into past generations that often influence the decisions someone will make.

This lesson was drummed into me, as I grappled with my ex-husband's inability to change even for the sake of our children—it was not possible for him to choose something that would stabilize our family, and I was unwilling to endure a pattern in our lives that was abusive and violent. The harder choice is the most challenging, and in this instance it was putting an end to the relationship, which I chose to do, although it brought me heavy financial burdens, and terrible guilt that I had not done enough to heal the marriage. Still, I moved on, taking on two and three jobs at a time to support my children, as their father simply refused to pay anything. Eventually, the State of Arizona would force some money out of him, however, this came unpredictably and for long periods of time, no money would come at all.

Amazingly, the internal world I had come to prize continued its existence in my life. Once the "okay" is given for internal growth to begin, it will continue throughout the life of a person, unless a person chooses to close the door to deeper understanding—and this I believe would be an exception to the rule. A "drink" from the refreshing waters that run through one's own soul is almost a guarantee that a person will find a way back to the center of self, where God's very image exists in quiet splendor. The silence and darkness within are the drawing cards. "Be still and know that I am God," (Psalm 46:10) are not merely ancient words, but a command meant to bring us into a reality that crosses lines of immortality. Our immortal life begins here and now, not at some later date. We begin "heaven," or "hell," on earth, long before we transition into spiritual beings.

Juggling Manuscripts

Rushing upon us, as writers, is always the next manu-script, the next place we will "live in" as we listen intently to the writer within for direction. Our outer life goes on with all its problems and challenges, and the quiet life within calls to us with the next idea, the next thing in our world that attracts our attention. I found that it is indeed possible to work on two books at a time, and have several "irons in the fire," which are multiple ideas and themes for future plans.

On February 17, 2007, as I waited for publication of my third book, *If I Die in Juárez*, I had a dream of having a baby while discovering another baby was due! I was told that the two babies would grow together. New baby dreams, such as seeing a baby, giving birth to a baby, holding an infant, etc., bring a message of newness, and of new beginnings. The "new baby dream" I had was correct, I would publish *If I Die in Juárez*, as my fourth book, in 2008, while *Women Who Live in Coffee Shops and Other Stories*, would be awarded the Chicano/Latino Literary Prize from the University of California at Irvine in the same year. Indeed, the "two babies" did grow together, and *Women Who Live in Coffee Shops and Other Stories* was released in 2010. There is often an overlapping in any act of creation, as ideas, images and "secret inklings," link with one another, crossing imaginary lines within, and keeping us on our toes, alert for the connections that bring more meaning to our lives and to our work. I would say, stay with your work to the end, unless you have been given the "green light" to move on to another work. Eventually, each writer grows to understand the "green" and "red" lights within, signaling the beginning and the end of a manuscript.

A Warning

I recall giving up on *Women Who Live in Coffee Shops*, at one point as I felt stuck, and could not seem to come up with more stories to add to the collection. The stories were written over a span of thirteen years before they were published, and I found myself adding one story or another, or submitting a story to a contest as a single piece. At one point, I even became "angry" with the work, and made up my mind to quit adding stories. That night, I felt relieved in a strange and reckless manner. I was grown up, and my manuscripts would not rule my life, or so I thought! As I worked out on a weight machine, at the gym later that evening, suddenly, from deep within, came that still, small thought pattern, a revelation rose into my conscious mind, as real as the weights I was lifting over my head. Referring directly to my decision to stop all work on my story collection, came these words: *If you do this, you will learn how to abandon your work, and you will never finish anything.*

It took me a few seconds to put down the weights, and clear my head. What I had been told was the truth! I didn't want to hear it—but I respected the message's authenticity.

I felt as if the "writer within," was cautioning me. The decision was still mine, but a warning had been given. Starting and never finishing a manuscript is a deadly habit to form. That night, I remember coming home from the gym and going straight to my home office, pulling out the box with the stories all packed away in their individual folders, and opening up the document for the manuscript on my computer. I sat at my computer and began writing the stories again, and lo and behold, the stories, some of which would later garner national awards, began to "give themselves" up to me again. If we are faithful to our work, it, in turn, will be faithful to us.

Your writing also has its own stages of growth. At times, it will seem like an infant, truly a baby, as I saw in my dream, needing your attention almost at every moment, at times turning into a demanding "brat!" Then, it will appear as a growing adolescent, almost standing on its own, then once it is polished, it seems to achieve full stature, and can go out into the world independent of you. The quality of your work must stand on its own. I often find that once my work is out in the publishing world, it doesn't seem to belong to me, exclusively. I read reviews and critiques about my work, and it is as if I am reading about the work of another author; almost as if my work is not mine alone, but belongs to every human being who has found meaning in its content. One thing is certain; a book will outlive its author, and bring meaning to readers long after the writer has ceased to exist on earth. Such is the power of the printed word.

Charged Spaces

Childhood memories of 7th Avenue and Van Buren in Phoenix took on a life of their own in *Women Who Live in Coffee Shops and Other Stories*. Our family home was located south of Buckeye Road, just north of I-17, which was one of the first freeways built to transverse the Valley, north to south. Van Buren was the street that separated the "haves," from the "have-nots," in other words for many years, land on the north side of Van Buren had greater property value than land on the south side of Van Buren. To the north, only blocks from my family home, lived the majority of Anglos who had established themselves via economic and educational success in communities that were well-maintained and considered middle to high income. Van Buren was the dividing line, between the rich and poor, a street such as all cities possess, yet over the years the "line" became less distinct as families of all nationalities moved into Phoenix, gaining strength through education and higher salaried jobs.

Van Buren was a thoroughfare for people traveling to Arizona from other states, especially California, New Mexico, and Texas. It became a "Las Vegan strip" of sorts, with hundreds of fancy, and not so fancy motels and hotels dotting both sides of the street, with bright neon lights announcing the: Tropics, Kon Tiki, Sandman, Coconut Grove, and the Ramada Inn, to name a few. Tovrea Castle on Van Buren, shaped like a wedding cake, was bought in the 1920's by Edward Tovrea, an eccentric entrepreneur who sought to attract "high-rollers," and dubious characters to Phoenix who might have connections to the underworld, and plenty of cash to spend in Phoenix. The castle didn't keep any of the high-rollers for long, as the stock-yards with over 35,000 head of cattle were just across the street, and the smell of cattle dung made the rich and famous hold their noses in disgust and take the first flight out of the city.

Van Buren's history included tales of the insane asylum called the "Green House," or in Spanish, *La Casa de los Locos*, (The Crazy House) which housed Arizona's infamous "trunk murderess," Winnie Ruth Judd, accused of slicing up her two girlfriends in a mad rage, possibly over a man. Many believed her innocent, yet her crime terrified the entire city, and instead of giving her the death penalty, she was sent to the insane asylum. I grew up with such stories, and many of them were directly related to the history of Van Buren Street.

Van Buren lives on in my memory as a "charged space," In other words, it is a place that evokes strong memories, scenes and characters. A charged space can be anywhere in your memory, or in your current life that has impacted you, or that brings about sensations, emotions, and images that at times play in your mind like videos.

Brainstorming Characters and Charged Spaces

One of the ways I begin a writing workshop is by first having participants brainstorm people known to them, at least five to ten, then circling the name that "jumps out at them," as I describe the creative writing process. They write about the person, using sensory descriptions, e.g., telling what the person wore, how they talked, what they said and did. They can also tell how they felt about the person—loving, angry, hurt, etc. These I call "believable characters," as they already hold a presence in the writer's mind. With a few changes here and there, the "believable characters" can develop into intricate protagonists who will attract readers with their authenticity. My work is filled with character traits seen in family members and friends, yet disguised in characters who still possess a distinct personality.

An extension of this exercise is to create a list of random names, at least five to ten of people whom the writer does *not* know. Be sure that they are truly random names, as once a real name is used, the writer tends to see the "real" person, instead of allowing a new character to come into being. The process is the same, circle the one that "jumps out at you." Write about that person, for instance:

Lynette was the kind of person who liked to dress up for work, even though everyone else went casual. She looked at herself in the mirror every day and searched her face for wrinkles, wondering if she would ever need plastic surgery. She often looked at movie magazines and compared herself to the women she saw there, fussing with her hair, using hair dye to make it blond or to become a brunette, making silent pledges to herself to "look like a million."

This sketch of "Lynette" was written "on the spot" so to speak, to give you an example of what it means to *create* new characters. With a little imagination you could create scenes, dialogue, and a plot that would unfold in Lynette's life given her obsession with "looking like a million." It is fascinating how many characters live within writers! Often, I will ask a group of writers if they knew the new characters they just created before the workshop began, and they will admit that they did not. Now they have fresh, new characters that can fit into short stories or novels. Almost every single character I have ever created is sketched out in this manner. A writer must know what color of socks their character prefers, or which candy bar he/she would choose at a vending machine. It is small details that make characters come to life for readers.

Brainstorming charged spaces is another very effective activity. I ask writers to list five to ten spaces they remember, e.g., the family kitchen, the neighborhood bakery, a park, a church, etc. and describe them physically, as well as telling who was there. Then they go one step further and tell about deep memories related to the charged space. One caution on this: If something brings great pain, do not feel obligated to write about it. If unable to write about a very painful memory, *leave it alone*. Perhaps, at another time, you will find yourself strong enough to address the person or charged space in your memory. Charged spaces can easily turn into settings for characters, and open the way for scenes, dialogue and memories that belong to the characters you have created. Yes, your characters will also have their own memories, created by *you*.

Reliving Van Buren Street

Van Buren was a huge "charged space," for me and the anchor story of the collection, "Women Who Live in Coffee

Shops," brought up the coffee shop I remembered on 7th Avenue and Van Buren: Helsing's. The coffee shop was sold many years ago, and eventually the building was demolished and now there is a McDonald's where the old coffee shop once stood.

In my mind's eye I could see the coffee shop, clearly, and visited the location to spark my memories. It is important for me to visit sites whenever possible, to confirm my memories, and draw energy from the actual places seen in my mind. In the story, Sal, a "retired Mafioso," is the owner of Sal's Coffee Shop, Andrea is his faithful waitress and eventually his business partner, and her nine-year old daughter, Joanna, tells the story of the adventures of the women who visit at the coffee shop. Using a child narrator to tell a story is a HIGHLY effective technique and can bring a perspective that is both entertaining and very endearing. Through Joanna's eyes we see the fancy motels now with faded walls, and chipped paint after years of use, some, with yellow spots in arcs that look like horseshoes on walls facing alleys. Joanna knew these were made by winos who used the walls as an outdoor bathroom. Joanna saw spots and stains in Sal's kitchen too that looked like huge eyes, but Sal didn't seem to mind as the health inspector from the City was a close friend of his and didn't have the heart to write up Sal on any code violations. Sal's Coffee Shop was a magnet, a place where the "invisible" people of the city were seen and heard, and where they mingled with one another welcomed by Sal's boisterous, giving spirit—and Andrea's need for the sisters she had always craved.

Ponder, Question, and Reflect

Every book you will write will have questions for you to ponder. The questions may not come at the beginning of a collection of stories, and maybe not even in the middle, but somewhere along the line, you will realize that the stories you are writing match in ways you could have never imagined. My questions for this collection centered around the concept of "invisibility." The book is dedicated to all the invisible city dwellers of the world, with the understanding that someday we will all be invisible.

I am fascinated by how a city gives "psychological permission," for a segment of its population to become invisible. The characters of *Women Who Live in Coffee Shops and Other Stories*, are invisible phantoms, flashy divas, addicts, mafiosos, mystics, hookers, bag ladies, criminals, transvestites, witches, priests-gone-wrong, illegals, and children who know too much---too soon. They are heart-broken, heart-breakers who are unafraid to laugh at life's tragic mishaps and open their lives to the humorous, ironic, dizzying life of the city's down-and-outers. I became determined to tell their stories.

I asked myself: Where do we reveal who we really are? Where do any of us feel safe telling our inmost thoughts, and most of all sharing our souls? In a city bustling with activity, coffee shops seem to be a place where people meet to talk. I often meet with people at coffee shops to discuss writing projects, world events, new books, business deals, on and on. The women in the main story find solace at Sal's, and sense they can be who they are without fear.

The concept of an, *anmchara*, defined by the ancient druids as a soul friend, came to my mind after several stories had been written, as I realized that no matter how "modern" we think we are, we all still need a true soul friend. The desire to share deeply the human experience is especially real for women, who seem to crave the internal connection, at times more passionately than men do. According to Joanna's mother, Andrea, Sal's was a good spot for the women—where else could they go—to bars where they would be suspected of being sluts and drunks? Society's judgment, at times, can be quite rigid.

The women who frequented Sal's became a family to Andrea, who had always wanted sisters, but was destined to be an only child. Joanna was also an only child, and shared the friendship of the ladies who were part of the, "League of Women Who Live in Coffee Shops," as she called her mother's band of women. The women formed a tight circle of friendship, and stood together against City Hall when Sal was investigated for his role in a murder case named, "The Sicilian Diamond Heist." The power of the women, all worried about the same thing at the same time, proved to be a combination that could not be dismantled in the story. My own upbringing in a house of seven girls and only one boy, certainly led me to realize the power of women when they decide to do something that has deep meaning for them—they are unstoppable.

Another story, "Devil in the Tree," deals with my own personal memory of a young boy who fell from a tree at Harmon Park in my old *barrio* and died. I had to pass by the tree on my way to my 8th grade class at Lowell School, and each time I looked at the tree, I felt a cold chill run through my body, and I would invariably begin to run.

The protagonists in the story, two children, Inocente and Sarita were caught up in an adult web of misunderstanding and accusations. Inocente, the older brother of the boy who had fallen to his death, was accused of murdering his own brother by not watching him as he had been told to do. Through a series of frightening and touching scenes, Sarita defended her friend, and finally came to the conclusion at the end of the story that what she had feared for so many years was *not* the tree. She now had to choose what to believe, and in a rare meeting between the two, the reader shares an intimate look at the richness of young love—new and astounding.

Another story deals with the memories of my gay cousin, who was as close to me as a brother. In "Ol' Lady Renteria," a sister comes to terms with her brother's life as a gay man. In this story I recalled all my cousin had been through; the vulgar words he was called, the beatings he received, and his early death at the age of twenty-six. A gentle man, his story lives on in Chan and his sister Mercedes as they piece their lives back together again after the death of their mother.

In this collection, I sought to use irony, humor and child narrators to define the mysterious combination of emotions, thoughts and insane choices that define us all as "imperfect people." I often tell creative writing students: "We're imperfect people, living in an imperfect world, telling our imperfect stories—and that's the charm." In fact, if they know someone who claims to be "perfect," I tell them I would rather *not* make that person's acquaintance!

The "hard-pressed" characters in the collection find ways to heal, bloom and at times completely change who they are. They are chameleons changing colors to fit into an urban city life that is edgy and out-of-control. Readers walk right into their lives, sharing some of my own memories, hidden in colorful, daring characters.

Identifying Your Own "Van Buren's"

Margaret, Queen of Scotland, the bag-lady in the collection, considered herself a descendant of royalty from Scotland, and is one of the many characters who will disarm readers with the essence of who they are, the secret beings that live in the weary, at times drug addicted and deformed misfits that tug at the heartstrings of readers and bring up memories of their own Van Buren Streets. Margaret was a friend to Sal, Andrea and Joanna, and offers readers a unique look at her own existence before she became a bag lady in the last story of the collection, "Enemy Lines."

Margaret was a homeless person who couldn't seem to make doctors, nurses, and cops understand that she really was sick, and not binging on alcohol. Her neighbor in the tattered apartment building she lived in, Gertie, was a transgender who had changed from woman to man, and was the only one to offer her genuine love and care. At one point, she hassled with the medical staff at Phoenix Memorial Hospital, especially with Marion, a vindictive nurse who often insulted Margaret and threatened her with the police. Margaret was finally escorted out of the hospital by a young, Mexican cop who reminded her of an old lover she had once lived with in Mexico City. The cop offered his arm as they walked out of the hospital and Margaret was grateful as she was truly ill—dizzy and disoriented. Upon walking out on the street she commented on the fact that it was a rainy night, and it reminded her of London. Incredulous, the young cop asked her when she had lived in London, and she mumbled that she had lived there as a child. Memories of her life in London and of her mother, a descendant of Scottish Highlanders, brought the past into stark reality for Margaret.

On her death bed, Margaret, unable to speak, began to recall her teen boyfriend, Alvin, and her mother, Mrs. Claybourne, as the social worker, Troy Hallerman, from the State Department asked question after question, appalled at the squalor she lived in. Margaret looked at the man, and saw in his face her old boyfriend, Alvin, and in the midst of her death experience, she relived the tragic love they had experienced as teenagers, and the baby she had been forced to put up for adoption. Now, the man who sat at her side, calling paramedics, had become her boyfriend, Alvin, come to play a prank on her...stop her from breathing as he dug his fingers into her throat. The social worker considered the old woman un-kept, and demented, not knowing that his link to her, had he known, forged a tie that would be rooted in the mystery of his own birth.

The tragic, yet true-to-life story of Margaret Queen of

Scotland, is the epitome of "invisibility," as the so-called educated and sane turn their backs on the old, alcoholic, not realizing her story was true. It reminds us that given a new set of circumstances from birth, or through wrong choices, anyone of us could become, "invisible," and walk in her shoes.

Not Everyone Who Should Love You, Will Love You

Another child narrator appears in the first story, "Benny," as Maria, an eight-year-old, searches for her drug-addicted father. The story won three major awards and was short-listed in the *Fish Anthology*, (1998) an Irish journal and recognized by Frank McCourt of *Angela's Ashes* as one of the best stories in a huge assortment of stories selected from around the world. In the story, Maria came to the conclusion that her dad was one of the characters who walked down Van Buren Street, she just didn't know which one, until one day while playing with her friends, Elida and Santigo in an abandoned warehouse.

A man watched them through a broken window, and the children became nervous and decided to climb out of the window and run home. As Maria climbed out last, the man took her hand and spoke to her in a friendly way, tousling her hair and calling her by name, telling her, Lisa, Maria's babysitter had told him her name. He knelt in front of his daughter, and put his hand flat against hers, and Maria noticed their hands were the same, except hers were smaller and cleaner. He told her he had been a piano player, and that she was one as well—the slender shape of her fingers proved it.

This story brings to light the tangled relationship of an absent father, and a daughter who deeply wanted to know him. In counseling teens, I have often heard many of them relate that they do not know their fathers. This sense of loss at times may deprive a youth from developing a healthy positive self-image.

Later, Maria discovered still another secret, much more potent. Her mother, outraged at her daughter meeting her father on Van Buren Street, punished her daughter, then after her rage was over, she sat with her daughter, and finally told her about her father's life. Maria asked her the one question all children want to know: Do you still love him? And her mother's answer, after a long pause, unveiled the truth—"Yes."

How can we still love someone who has deeply hurt us? How do we make sense of someone who cannot love back? I have often counseled people: *Not everyone who should love you, will love you. Now what?* The challenge is there. Do we fight for someone's love, or do we come to terms with the truth that love is freely given and freely received. No one *owes* us love. And we cannot expect love from someone who is incapable of first loving self. Love is a complicated force to contemplate, and in the eyes of an eight year-old, the fact that her mother still loved her missing dad was enough to begin a healing.

Sexual Exploitation

Coming to the forefront in this collection was another preoccupation of mine, a huge concern that will be the basis of a future book: the sexual prostitution of children, world-wide. This theme showed up in the story, "One of These Days I'm Gonna Go Home," the story of Buzzard, a one-armed vet of the Korean War, and his sister, Peggy, who was determined to adopt an orphan from Mexico to offer the child, the "abundant life," as promised by Christ in his teachings. Peggy made the trip to Nogales, Mexico in spite of her brother's opposition, and ignored the Mexican pastor's warning against adopting eleven year-old Emma who had been used as a prostitute in the underground tunnels dug illegally between Nogales and the U.S.

A series of horrific events took place as soon as Emma arrived in Phoenix. Neighbors even suspected that the child had been brought to America for Buzzard—as if he could somehow own the child. Buzzard was fascinated by Emma, and at the same time afraid of his own feelings towards a child who had been sold as a prostitute. Alarmed at how Mexican men looked at Emma, Buzzard yelled at his sister, claiming she had brought dangerous men into their lives after learning that Emma's father had been a notorious drug-trafficker. Convinced that he must do something to protect the girl and his sister, Buzzard gave up his idea of going back to New York, as he had always threatened: one of these days he would go home, and no one would stop him. Now, he knew those words had been a lie. All his life he had lied to himself.

In the end Buzzard, Peggy and Emma shared a life together that would have seemed impossible, and not the abundant life Peggy had envisioned, but one filled with Emma's determination to go to school, and Buzzard's new role as a protector. Buzzard was running around with a revolver at his hip, while Peggy was teaching Emma how to read. By then, Emma had cut her hair like a boy, attended school everyday, and shunned all men—not the abundant life Peggy had imagined. The dark, yet at times, ironic look at life's tragedies strengthened the collection as it brought hope to the worst darkness imaginable, and made heroes of the "invisible people."

Follow the trail of your memories. They will bring to mind fantastic scenes, characters and plots long forgotten that will spring into life once they know *you* are interested. Your own questions will lead the way as you watch closely what it is that attracts your attention. Simply search within, sifting through your memories, so many of them. Which ones are calling to you? Dreams may come, visions within dreams, revelations, and blurry places no longer in existence. These are good signs: the power of story is upon you. You have only to listen deeply, let the characters form in your mind, create the "charged spaces," which will become new locations, perhaps exotic places filled with strange and wondrous beings, and you will become their scribe.

9

THE CALL TO WRITE

Keep the barking dogs off the estate.
Letters of the Scattered Brotherhood

OFTEN people at conferences, classes or in workshops tell me they want to write, but they will have to wait until their kids are all out of school, or their parents are no longer ill, or once they sell their house...on and on—the excuses are many. I wish I could say that life will offer you plenty of time to write. Nothing difficult will come your way, and you will not experience pain, sorrow, or the death of a loved one. But, that would truly be a fairy tale! Life will continue to send you daily challenges, some of them so dark and problematic, they may cause depression, or sickness, or a sense of futility—why should I write? The question plagues writers everywhere. Life's relentless pace is at times, unmerciful, and many writers, who should be producing work, are undone by trials and produce nothing. Why do *you* write?

It is a good idea to ask yourself why you are writing, even if the answer is, "I don't know." I had a writer call me recently to ask my advice on a memoir she was finishing up. She could not tell me much about her work, except that other people liked it. She had gotten feedback from a few people and was happy that the feedback had been positive. She had not yet found a publisher or an agent. I asked her again to describe her work, and she repeated a vague description. Her main concern seemed to be how much money she could expect from the book, and I had no answer for that.

It is crucial for writers to be able to describe what they are writing, both in a longer synopsis, chapter by chapter, in summary, in a nutshell, and often as a one-liner. That's how well a writer needs to know what their work is about. An editor or publishing house will ask for all kinds of descriptions, as they want to view the work through several perspectives. Self-publishing carries the same amount of responsibility, and at times, even greater accountability, as a writer often becomes his or her own copy editor. Whether self-published or publishing through an agency or publishing house, you would be surprised how much marketing must be done by the writer before the book ever hits the printing press. The target audience must also be known, and ways to reach the audience. Who will buy the book, and why? What would you, a publishing house, or an agent gain from producing the work? Writers must be ready to answer, and do their own research, detailing people, organizations, affiliations, schools, and possible contacts for media, and others who might have an interest in the book.

In the end, the publishing industry, like any other business is driven by profits—the bottom line is money. University presses, and some smaller presses often will take on a writing project because they see its worth in the community, school setting, or as a work of art. I felt fortunate that, *If I Die in Juárez*, was published by the University of Arizona Press, as they are highly regarded for producing works related to the Southwest, and to social issues that affect the broader world community. Just as anticipated, the book attracted high schools, colleges and universities. I have presented to numerous women studies programs, human rights conferences, and book groups concerned about the "crime of the century." This audience has brought me many new readers from coast to coast, as well as from abroad, and the interest continues to hold.

The big houses usually look first at how a book will profit their house, and if it is a good fit for their marketing plans and future goals. If a writer is driven by profits, alone, I would advice that person to rethink why they are writing. We write because we must, because to *not* write would be to stop an internal process that is as natural as breathing. Writing becomes a part of our daily lives, it is everywhere, we think in images, photographic memories live on in our minds like still-life's. A writer can be on an airplane, or train, in an exclusive restaurant, or on a busy city street, and see potential characters everywhere. Ideas are abundant and free for the taking. I often laugh with my students in creative writing classes as I describe stopping at a busy intersection, and sometimes coming up with several scenes for stories, depending on what's going on, before the light turns green!

How Do You Deal With "Barking Dogs?"

Once you discover your own writing life, like anything else that you cherish, you will want to guard it with vigilance. *Letters From the Scattered Brotherhood*, gives us a strong sense of what this means in the words: *Keep the barking dogs off the estate.* Whatever it is that disturbs your balance, that causes you to fragment and be swayed by emotional ups and downs has the potential of become a "barking dog."

At the time I am writing these words, I have just answered an emergency call for a pressing family matter, which both frightens me and brings me feelings of deep hopelessness. There is nothing I can do at this point to rescue the person involved, yet this extreme situation going on in my family causes me great internal pain. Adding to my painful family matter is the death of a beloved member of our community, and several other matters that weigh heavily on my heart. My question is this: Should I stop my work at this point? Should I sound a horn of despair, wring my hands, or shed tears? To do any of these things would solve absolutely nothing. Tears are good, and I shed those when I need to, and I pray, and often talk to dear friends who can offer me their support and kind words. BUT THE WRITING MUST GO ON! I compare it to a marriage vow: for better or for worse, in sickness and in health, until death, do us part. Divorce is not an option. How can you divorce the deepest part of who you are?

I recall when writing the last story of *Fragile Night*, my younger daughter, Deborah, decided to board a bus with one of her cousins, and join her in a day of playing "hookey," from high school, and running around with friends. It was absolutely unnerving for me as I searched for her in league with school officials, then on my own as evening drew near. Finally, I settled on staying up all night, and writing one of the most powerful stories of the collection, "Once for Pepito," the story of a young boy dying of cancer.

Pepito's last wish was to ride on the back of a whale. His mother and uncle were determined to grant him his last wish, although neither had a clue as to how the child's wish would come true. They took him to the ocean that was a few hours away, as Pepito struggled for every breath, sitting between the two adults in his uncle's old pick-up truck. They had hoped that perhaps Pepito would catch a glimpse of a whale in the distant ocean; however life had a surprise in store for them.

Unknown to the three, a whale was beached on the shore. Upon arriving Tío Sabio jumped out of his pick-up truck and ran through the crowd of on-lookers with his young nephew in his arms, and Pepito's mother, Angelica, close behind. In a magical and powerful moment, Pepito's wish was granted. As his uncle pressed close to the whale, Pepito touched the whale's glistening head, so unlike his own lacerated one. Death reached for him, and a glorious smile appeared on his face. It is then, that the reader takes off with Pepito on his joyous ride on the back of the whale; a ride once coveted by every boy in the whole world, now belongs to Pepito *and* to the reader. This is magical realism.

This story became part of the literary curriculum for over 500 teens at Metro Tech High School in Phoenix this past semester. The students were studying magical realism, and were charmed by the child, Pepito, and his wondrous wish. They created their own stories, using magical realism, and also painted a mural with Pepito in the center, riding on a whale, and the characters of their own stories flanking Pepito's story on either side. It is now a permanent exhibit in one of the school's front lobbies. Often, great pain can bring about great beauty that will connect powerfully with others and remain a part of our human experience for years to come.

And what about my daughter who ran away that fateful night? Her absence led me to the center of my own pain and to Pepito's story. She not only completed high school, but went on to graduate from the W.P. Carey School of Business at Arizona State University, and is now a Mom to my two beautiful granddaughters! Every time we salute love, and live out the purpose of our lives, we will, in the end, find enrichment beyond our wildest dreams.

Happiness vs. Joy

I have found that desiring happiness is not enough. Happiness is an illusion. It is here today, and gone the next minute. We may wake up in a happy mood, then receive news that shatters our sense of well-being, and our whole life grows dark. I have come to realize that what I desire is JOY, yes, joy, a deep sense that rises from my very being that tells me all is well with my soul. I can bravely face whatever life has in store for me if my soul is at peace. That is where the "private estate" exists for each of us. That is what must be protected at all costs, and the "barking dogs" driven off. No, we cannot stop bad things from happening, nor put an end to things that give us pain, but we can stand guard over our hearts, be ever vigilant, and make sure our "private estate" within is still controlled by one of the most powerful forces on earth: *our free will.*

One thing I have found helpful, is to do a series of "heart checks," throughout the day. I am not referring to monitoring a beating heart or checking blood pressure, I am referring to a turning within, which can be done in an instant, and a quick check on what's going on in my own internal world. Often, surrounded by hundreds of people at book signings, or in the midst of a family celebration, or at a conference, or perhaps alone in my own home as I sense myself becoming scattered and painful thoughts rising or feel myself sensing a negative feeling towards a person, or to what someone has said, I turn quickly within. No one notices, yet for me, this turning within is the very life-line of who I am.

Over the years, I have become determined to look internally, not outwardly as I used to do in the past, and in this way I can put my "house in order," without delay. I ask myself questions. Does the person who irritated me remind me of someone? Am I responding to something that brings up a bitter memory? Am I tired and in need of rest? Do I feel overlooked, and frustrated at being seen as insignificant? Once I zero in on what is causing the disharmony, I am ready to deal with the "barking dogs." People have asked me in workshops, "But isn't this tiring? Heart checks all day long seem so hard to do!" Then

I explain that heart checks are easy to do compared to things such as: losing your heart to someone who was not worthy of you, and spending your life in the wrong relationship, or in a job you hate; nurturing a bitter memory, or not completing something that was good for you. All these things can consume a lifetime. Then, as the person *comes to terms with the dark parts of who they are*, they must go back to the sixteen year old who ran away from home, or to the young man who fought so bitterly with his father and never had a chance to ask for forgiveness. Now, they must bring that young person back home again as the human spirit is one, and cannot exist in fragments. That's hard.

I like to take the easy way out, run towards the pain, meet it as it comes around the corner, ready to face whatever dark time it represents, look at it full-face and be tender and gentle to the young woman caught so many years in a hopeless marriage. Feel for her, her anguish, and not accuse her of being "stupid," and "ignorant." I actually had to go back into all the terrible memories that had been so destructive over the years, and forgive the young woman I had been who had committed so many failings, and bring her home in triumph!

I have found that the way you treat the parts of who you are, is the way you will treat others. An angry person will treat others with anger. A hateful person will see hate everywhere. An impatient person will have little patience with self or others. The way you deal with your internal world reflects in how you choose to deal with your external world. I caution people with the age-old phrase: "Watch what you pray for." I have heard people tell me they prayed for patience, and chaotic things began to happen, one after another. "Now what?" they ask me. I tell them, "Your prayers have been answered. How will you learn patience if you're not tested? How will you develop the integrity to hold on to patience if your "soul's muscles" are not exercised by the things that can build resiliency and stamina?"

What Do You Cherish?

The philosopher, William James, once said: "The things we cherish most, are at the mercy of the things we cherish least." As writers, we must figure out what we cherish, what we value in our lives, and what we would stand for against all odds. I will never forget the "silent thanks," I experienced as Mom's death rushed upon her. Mom had slipped into a coma and could no longer speak in an audible voice, yet as I knelt at her bedside, looking intently into her eyes, she spoke to me in the mysterious language of the soul. As simply as if we were having a conversation at the kitchen table over coffee, these words formed themselves in my mind: *Thank you, mija, for bringing me to your house*. The words were said in Spanish, *Gracias, mija por traerme a tu casa*, and this heightened their effect on me, as Spanish was the language of my childhood. I answered, also in Spanish: "It was a privilege and an honor to have you in my home," and with that, my mother took her last breath and peacefully left her body. It was not until much later that I sought to make sense of what had happened—the easy way Mom's words had reached me so profoundly, and materialized in my mind as a "whole," as if placed there in a single instant. This is the language of the spirit, instantaneous speech that transcends our clumsy use of words.

I deeply cherished my relationship with my mother, father and other family members, yet as William James has pondered, often what we cherish most is at the mercy of what we cherish least. We cherish family, and we make little time to spend with them. We cherish peace and we are at war. We cherish giving, yet have no time to exercise the act of giving—on an on. The things we cherish most are in peril.

Mom left several things in my home that were very personal to her, among them a ring (onyx and silver), a hair brush, mirror, a prayer book etched with scribbled words, and one of the aprons she herself had created. I cherish these things, as they belonged to someone who loved me unconditionally. I did not have to prove anything to Mom to win her love—it simply was there for me. Her ring showed up on one of two huge billboards that were put up in the middle of downtown Phoenix when *Let Their Spirits Dance*, was published. I didn't have the nerve to approach the billboard with a photograph of myself I could see from a long way off—enormous. One day I forced myself to go look, and saw my hand, holding my book, and very clearly—there was Mom's onyx, silver ring! Then, I called my sister, Lupe to come look...I was seeing something I had cherished for so long, the ring Mom had left me, magnified many times over!

Mom's apron is another one of my cherished possessions. I have shown it at numerous classes, workshops, events, and conferences. It travels with me in my luggage everywhere

I go. Safety pins adorn its faded material as Mom always had a collection of safety pins available for her daughters who might need them at any point in time. Her advise to us was clear: "Never go out without a safety pin, something will tear or snap and you will be standing there—naked!" Amusing words, but very true. There have been several times when Mom's safety pins have come to my rescue when traveling in various cities. On the apron's pocket is another safety pin, holding a loop of red rubber bands—in case we were cooking by the stove and needed to keep our hair out of the fire.

Mom's apron reminds me of a beautiful woman who only went up to the 3rd grade in elementary school. Disenfranchised from the "American dream," she nonetheless cultivated her own soul, and taught me how to do the same. Her apron tells of unconditional love, and her untiring desire to serve her family in the minutest details of life: safety pins and rubber bands!

What is priceless in your life? What is it that you would not sell at *any* price? The things you name will define who you are. They are your treasures, and are a roadmap to your heart. Identify the things you cherish, within yourself and within the characters you create.

Your life as a writer depends on your making time to write, learning the workings of your internal world, and defining your own revelations, visions and dreams. Writing skills can come through classes and practice, but no one can lead you *within*, except yourself. Deciphering the voice of your own soul involves a lifetime of listening to quiet inner communications that can be so easily disregarded in the loud, noisy world. You will encounter "private wars," times when it will seem as if you are fighting with a manuscript, or at war with things in your life that bring you sorrow and pain. Yet, it is these times that, if you allow, will lead you steadily into the invisible world, the heart of your own creative energy. There you will discover the language of your own soul, rich and magnanimous, and it will form brilliant pathways—guiding you on your own miraculous writing journey.

Made in the
USA
Columbia, SC